Y0-BSE-021

SPEAK ENGLISH

A Practical Course
for Foreign Students

Marie Durel

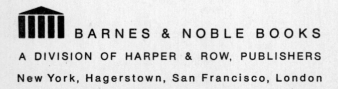

BARNES & NOBLE BOOKS

A DIVISION OF HARPER & ROW, PUBLISHERS

New York, Hagerstown, San Francisco, London

First BARNES & NOBLE BOOKS edition published 1972.

LIBRARY OF CONGRESS CATALOG CARD NUMBER: 72–161238.

STANDARD BOOK NUMBER: 06–463320–9

2 83 84 85 86   10 9 8

PREFACE

"How long will it take me to learn to speak English?" That is the question the teacher hears most often, and there are as many different answers as there are different students.

The answer depends on the student's ability and language aptitude, but it also depends upon many other factors—the amount of time he can devote to study and oral practice, his opportunities for listening to the target language, the materials he studies, and the exercises he performs; and, yes, some of it depends upon his teacher.

The student who has the patience and perseverance to spend hours in oral repetition, repeating the same sentence aloud many times while concentrating upon its meaning, will be the first one to acquire fluency in the new language.

But "fluency" is a relative term. In using these lessons, I expect my students to be "fluent," within limits of course, after sufficiently practicing the very first lesson. That is, in the material covered by Lesson I, they must be truly fluent before going on to Lesson II.

This text only lays the foundation for vocabulary building. The alert student will pick up new words daily. These lessons provide him with a basic vocabulary of about a thousand words. To these he must add several thousand more which he will gain from reading and listening.

It has been my experience that if the student acquires skill in the use of verbs, pronouns, and prepositions, the other elements in the sentence will fall into place. Familiarity with the use of these basic elements is to be followed, not preceded, by the acquisition of an adequate vocabulary.

These lessons are designed primarily to give the student an understanding of English sentence structure and to develop his skill in putting words and ideas together in an intelligible pattern—in other words, to make it possible for him to communicate his ideas. Words are his raw materials, the bricks and lumber and steel of the house he wants to build. Here are the building plans that will show him how to put them together.

TABLE OF CONTENTS

LESSON I

*Present Tense of **be**, Affirmative, Interrogative, and Negative—Articles, Definite and Indefinite—Subject Pronouns—Possessive Adjectives*

You will need a small dictionary showing English words and their meaning in the language that you speak. Look in your dictionary, and write the definitions of these words in your own language:

a, an[1] _____

the[2] _____

and _____

be _____

ready _____

office _____

busy _____

Subject Pronouns

SINGULAR		PLURAL	
I	_____	we	_____
you	_____	you	_____
he	_____	they	_____
she	_____		
it	_____		

Pronunciation

[1] A (ə) before a consonant: a man, a book
An (ən) before a vowel: an Indian, an old man
[2] The (ðə) before a consonant: the man, the book
The (ðɪ) before a vowel: the Indian, the old man

Present Tense of the Verb *Be**

Form 1	Form 2	Form 3
Affirmative	Interrogative	Negative
I am	am I?	I am not
you are	are you?	you are not
he is, she is, it is	is he? is she? is it?	he is not, she is not, it is not
we are	are we?	we are not
you are	are you?	you are not
they are	are they?	they are not

Exercise A.   First, do the entire exercise orally, asking the questions and repeating the answers. Then, write the answers in a notebook (there will not always be sufficient space in the text) and again repeat orally until questions and answers are automatic. Number the pages in your notebook to correspond with the pages in the text.

1. Are you ready?

Yes, I am ready.   No, I am not ready.

2. Is he ready?

Yes, he is ready.   No, he is not ready.

3. Is she ready?

Yes, _____ .   No, _____ .

4. Is it ready?

Yes, _____ .   No, _____ .

5. Are we ready?

Yes, _____ .   No, _____ .

6. Are they ready?

Yes, _____ .   No, _____ .

Exercise B.   Use *pronouns* in your answers to these questions:

1. Are you in New York?

Yes, I _____ .   No, _____ .

2. Is Henry in Chicago?

Yes, he _____ .   No, _____ .

*See also page 249, Appendix 1.

2

3. Is Margaret in
Miami?

Yes, she _____ .   No, _____ .

4. Is the office in
Chicago?

Yes, it _____ .   No, _____ .

5. Are you and
John in New
Orleans?

Yes, we _____ .   No, _____ .

6. Are John and
Betty in Paris?

Yes, they _____ .   No, _____ .

Again, repeat orally many times, changing the names of the cities.

Possessive Adjectives

Look in your dictionary and write the definitions of the possessive adjectives:

SINGULAR	PLURAL
my _____	our _____
your _____	your _____
his _____	their _____
her _____	
its _____	

New Words

friend _____	friends _____
brother _____	brothers _____
sister _____	sisters _____

Exercise C.

1. Are you busy?

Yes, _____ .   No, _____ .

2. Is your brother
busy?

Yes, my brother

_____ .

No, _____ .

3. Is your sister
busy?

Yes, _____ .

No, _____ .

4. Are you and your
brother busy?

Yes, we _____ .

No, _____ .

5. Are your friends
busy?

Yes, they _____ .

No, _____ .

These three exercises in Lesson I *must be practiced orally* many, many times, until you speak automatically and *think in English*.

Dialog

Is your brother in Washington?
Yes, he is in Washington now.
Are you and your sister busy while your brother is in Washington?
No, we are not very busy.
(The dialog is to be memorized and practiced as a conversation between two persons.)

LESSON II

Present Tense of the Verbs **work, take, go,**
and **have**—*Drill on Possessive Adjectives*

Four New Verbs

	airport _____	book _____
work _____	bank _____	college _____
take _____	car (automobile) _____	school _____
go _____	door _____	university _____
have _____	lessons _____	Saturday _____
	music _____	Sunday _____

Only a very few verbs are similar to **be** in the interrogative (Form 2) and the negative (Form 3). Almost all English verbs form the interrogative and negative with the auxiliary **do** or **does**. The verb form is the same in all persons, *with the exception of the 3d person singular.*

Present Tense of the Verb *Work**

FORM 1 AFFIRMATIVE	FORM 2 INTERROGATIVE	FORM 3 NEGATIVE
I work	do I work?	I do not work
you work	do you work?	you do not work
he *works*, she *works*, it *works*	*does* he work? *does* she work? *does* it work?	he *does* not work, she *does* not work, it *does* not work
we work	do we work?	we do not work

*See also page 254, Appendix 1.

5

Form 1	Form 2	Form 3
Affirmative	Interrogative	Negative
you work	do you work?	you do not work
they work	do they work?	they do not work

Exercise A. Using subject pronouns, answer the following questions in the affirmative (Form 1):

1. Do you work on Saturday?   Yes, I work on Saturday.
2. Does Henry work on Sunday?   Yes, he *works* on Sunday.
3. Does Betty work on
Saturday?   Yes, _____ .
4. Do you and Frank work at
the airport?   Yes, _____ .
5. Do Henry and John work at
the bank?   Yes, _____ .

Using Form 3, answer the same questions in the *negative*:

No, I do not work on Saturday.

No, he *does not work* _____ .

No, she _____ .

No, we _____ .

No, they _____ .

Present Tense of the verb *Take*

Exercise B. Now we will use the verb **take,** which in the present tense has forms *exactly similar* to those you have learned for the verb **work.** Answer the following questions with "Yes" (Form 1):

1. Do you take English lessons?   Yes, I take _____ .

2. Does John take English lessons?   Yes, he *takes* _____ .

3. Does Helen take music lessons?   Yes, she _____ .

4. Do you and Betty take
French lessons?   Yes, we _____ .

5. Do Helen and Betty take
Spanish lessons?   Yes, they _____ .

Using Form 3, answer the same questions in the *negative:*

No, I do not take _____ .

No, he *does not take* _____ .

No, she _____ .

No, we _____ .

No, they _____ .

The other verbs in this lesson are similar, in the present tense, to **work** and **take.**

Present Tense of the Verb *Go*

Exercise C. The verb **go** is irregular in the spelling of the 3d person singular of the affirmative (Form 1): *he goes, she goes, it goes.*

1. Do you go to the university?

Yes, I go _____ .
No, I do not go ____ .

2. Does Henry go to school?

Yes, he goes _____ .
No, he does not go

_____ .

3. Does Grace go to college?

Yes, _____ .
No, _____ .

4. Do you and your brother go to college?

Yes, we _____ .
No, _____ .

5. Do your brother and sister go to school?

Yes, they _____ .
No, _____ .

Present Tense of the Verb *Have*

Exercise D. The verb **have** is also irregular in the 3d person singular of the affirmative (Form 1): *he has, she has, it has.*

1. Do you have a car?

Yes, I have _____ .   No, I do not have

_____ .

    2. Does your
       brother have a
       car?

Yes, he *has* _____ .   No, he *does not have*

_____ .

    3. Does Mrs.
       Brown have a
       car?

Yes, she _____ .   No, _____ .

    4. Does the car
       have four doors?

Yes, it _____ .   No, _____ .

    5. Do you and your
       brother have a
       car?

Yes, _____ .   No, _____ .

    6. Do Mr. and Mrs.
       Brown have a
       car?

Yes, _____ .   No, _____ .

Possessive Adjectives

Exercise E.   Refer again to the possessive adjectives on page 3, and study their use in the following sentences:

    I go to *my* class.   She goes to *her* class.
    You go to *your* class.   We go to *our* class.
    He goes to *his* class.   They go to *their* class.

Complete the following sentences by filling in all blanks:

1. I have *my* book.   7. I take ___*my*___ lesson.

2. You have *your* book.   8. You take _____ lesson.

3. He *has* _____ book.   9. He *takes* _____ lesson.

4. She _____ _____ book.   10. She _____ _____ lesson.

5. We _____ _____ books.   11. We _____ _____ lesson.

8

6. They _____ _____ books.   12. They _____ _____ lesson.

Dialog

Does your brother go to college?
Yes, he goes to Brent College.
Does he have his books?
No, he doesn't have his books.

LESSON III

*Review Drills on Present Tense of the
Verbs **be, work,** and **take***

breakfast _____   eat   _____

lunch   _____   study   _____

dinner   _____   bookstore _____

supper   _____   post office _____

Exercise A.

1. Is breakfast ready?

Yes, it _____ .   No, _____ .

2. Is dinner ready?

Yes, _____ .   No, _____ .

Answer the following questions with "Yes."

3. Are you ready to go?   Yes, I am _____ .

4. Is John ready to eat lunch?   Yes, _____ .

5. Is Helen ready to study?   Yes, _____ .

6. Are you and Helen ready to eat supper?   Yes, _____ .

7. Are John and Helen ready to go?   Yes, _____ .

Using Form 3, answer the same questions with "No."

10

No, I am not ready to go.

No, he is not _____ .

No, she _____ .

No, we _____ .

No, they _____ .

From your dictionary, write definitions of the following words:

father	_____	farmer	_____
mother	_____	housewife	_____
uncle	_____	lawyer	_____
aunt	_____	nurse	_____
cousin	_____	salesman*	_____
accountant	_____	secretary	_____
businessman	_____	stenographer	_____
clerk	_____	storekeeper	_____
doctor	_____	student	_____
engineer	_____	teacher	_____

Exercise B.   Further drill on the present tense of **be.**

Are you a teacher?   No, I am not a teacher; I am a student.

Continue with answers in the same form, choosing an appropriate occupation for the second part of the question.

1. Are you a farmer?   No, I am not _____ ; I am _____ .

2. Is your brother a lawyer?   No, he _____ ; he _____ .

3. Is your uncle an engineer?   No, he _____ ; he _____ .

*Note that the plural of "salesman" is "salesmen."

11

4. Is Alice a secretary?   No, she _____ ; _____ .

5. Is your aunt a nurse?   No, _____ ; _____ .

6. Are you and Henry farmers?   No, we _____ ; we _____ .

7. Are John and Frank
   accountants?   No, _____ ; _____ .

8. Is your cousin a salesman?   No, he _____ ; _____ .

9. Are your cousins salesmen?   No, they _____ ; _____ .

Exercise C. Review the verb **work** in Lesson II, Forms 1, 2, and 3.

Do you work at the post   No, I do not work at the post
office?   office; I work at the bank.

Continue with answers in the same form, choosing a location.

1. Does your cousin work at the   No, he does not work at the
   bank?   bank; he works _____ .

2. Does your brother work at
   the airport?   No, _____ ; _____ .

3. Does Betty work at the hotel?   No, _____ ; _____ .

4. Do you and Henry work at
   the bookstore?   No, _____ ; _____ .

5. Do John and Frank work at
   the airport?   No, _____ ; _____ .

Exercise D. Review the verb **take** in Lesson II.

Continue with answers in the same form, choosing an appropriate means of transportation.

plane _____   train _____   bus _____   boat _____

Do you take the plane to   No, I do not take the plane to
Chicago?   Chicago; I take the bus.

1. Do you take the bus to
   Miami?   No, _____ ; _____ .

2. Does Olga take the train to   No, she does not _____ ;
   Tulsa?   she takes _____ .

3. Does Tom take the boat to
   Kingston?   No, _____ ; _____ .

4. Do you and Tom take the plane to St. Louis?   No, _____ ; _____ .
5. Do Mr. and Mrs. Hill take the bus to Denver?   No, _____ ; _____ .

Dialog

Does Henry take the train to Chicago?
No, he doesn't take the train; he takes the plane.
Is he ready to go to Chicago today?
Yes, he is ready to go.

LESSON IV

*Present Tense of the Verb **live**, with Local Streets and Avenues—Review Drills on the Verb **have** with Possessive Adjectives*

Write the names of three streets and three avenues in the city where you live now:

_____ Street _____ Avenue

_____ Street _____ Avenue

_____ Street _____ Avenue

live _____ parents _____ ticket _____

Exercise A.   The verb **live** follows the *same pattern* as **work** and **take**. Fill in the blanks in the following questions, and answer each question:

1. Do you live on _____ Street?   Yes, _____ .

2. Does Charles live on
_____ Street?   Yes, he *lives* _____ .

3. Does Miss Taylor live on
_____ Avenue?   Yes, _____ .

4. Do you and your parents
live on _____ Avenue?   Yes, _____ .

5. Do Mr. and Mrs. Smith
live on _____ Street?   Yes, _____ .

Using Form 3 of your model verb **work**, answer "No" to the same questions:

No, I do not live on _____ Street.

14

No, he *does not live* _____ .

No, she _____ .

No, _____ .

No, _____ .

Drills on the Verb *Have* with Possessive Adjectives

Exercise B. Review the verb **have** (Lesson II, pp. 7–8). Study the possessive adjectives in the same lesson. Then answer "Yes" to the following questions:

1. Do you have *your* tickets?　　Yes, I have *my* tickets.

2. Does Charles have *his* tickets?　　Yes, _____ .

3. Does Olga have *her* tickets?　　Yes, _____ .

4. Do we have *our* tickets?　　Yes, _____ .

5. Do Mr. and Mrs. Allen have *their* tickets?　　Yes, _____ .

Using Form 3, answer "No" to the same questions:

No, I do not have my tickets.

No, he _____ .

No, she _____ .

No, they _____ .

No, we _____ .

Exercise C.

with _____　　here _____

without _____　　there _____

1. I live with __(my)__ parents.　　7. I do not have __(my)__ car here.

2. You live with _(your)_ parents.　　8. You do not have __ car here.

3. He lives with _____ parents.

4. She _____.

5. We _____.

6. They _____.

9. He does not have

_____ car here.

10. She _____.

11. We _____.

12. They _____.

In *oral practice*, use the above sentences to answer the following questions. *Repeat many times orally.*

1. Whom do you live with?   I live with my parents.

2. Whom do I live with?   You _____.

3. Whom does John live with?   He _____.

4. Whom does Helen live with?   She _____.

5. Whom do you and your sister live with?   We _____.

6. Whom do John and his brother live with?   They _____.

7. Do you have your car here?   No, I _____.

8. Do I have my car here?   No, you _____.

9. Does John have his car here?   No, _____.

10. Does Helen have her car here?   No, _____.

11. Do you and your sister have your car here?   No, _____.

12. Do John and his brother have their car here?   No, _____.

Dialog

Is the theater on Franklin Street?
No, it is on Tenth Avenue.
Does Betty have her tickets for the show?
Yes, she has her tickets.

LESSON V

*Plural Forms of the Noun—**there is**, **there are**—**some**, **any**, **not any**—Uncountable Nouns—Verbal Contractions **isn't** and **aren't***

Write the definition of each singular noun, and study its plural form:

	REGULAR			IRREGULAR IN SPELLING	
boy	boys	_____	family	families[2]	_____
girl	girls	_____	baby	babies	_____
thing	things	_____	fly	flies	_____
table	tables	_____	penny	pennies	_____
house	houses	_____	life	lives	_____
dish	dishes[1]	_____	knife	knives	_____
box	boxes	_____	leaf	leaves	_____
	IRREGULAR				
man	men	_____			

---

[1] Words ending in *s*, *sh*, *ch*, or *x* add "es" to form the plural: dresses, wishes, matches, taxes.

[2] Final "y" *following a consonant* changes to "ie": lady, ladies; city, cities. Final "y" *following a vowel* does not change: play, plays; valley, valleys.

woman   women   _____

child   children _____

foot   feet   _____

tooth   teeth   _____

mouse   mice   _____

sheep   sheep   _____

In English, *only the noun* has a plural form. The adjective keeps the same form for masculine or feminine, singular or plural:

the *old* woman	the *old* man	the *old* house
the *old* women	the *old* men	the *old* houses

good _____   large _____   news _____

bad _____   small _____   people _____

"News" is always singular: The news *is* good. The news *is* bad.
"People" is always plural: The people *are* ready. The people *are* not ready.

Exercise A.   Change the subject noun to its plural form in the following sentences. Make the necessary change in the verb form:

1. The boy is not ready.   The boys are not ready.

2. The house is on Main Street.   The houses are _____ .

3. The baby is in the hospital.   _____ .

4. The man is busy.   _____ .

5. His foot is large.   _____ .

6. Her foot is small.   _____ .

7. The girl is in school.   _____ .

8. The woman is not here.   _____ .

18

9. The child is not there. _____.

10. The dish is on the table. _____.

11. The penny is in the box. _____.

12. The knife is here. _____.

There Is, There Are

Find the meaning of the following expressions in your dictionary:

	INTERROGATIVE	NEGATIVE
there is _____	is there?	there is not
		(there isn't)*
there are _____	are there?	(there aren't)*

Example: There is a fly on the table.

"There" is an anticipatory subject, representing the true subject "fly." The verb form—**is** or **are**—agrees in number with the true subject.

> *A fly* **is** on the table.
> There are ten children in the class.
> *Ten children* **are** in the class.

Some, Any, Not Any—Uncountable Nouns

There is (plural **there are**) is often followed by an expression of indefinite quantity—**some**. **Some** is used before plural nouns (*some boys*, i.e., an indefinite number of boys), or before nouns which usually do not have a plural form† (*some milk*, i.e., an indefinite quantity of milk).

The following rules apply to **some** and **any** *when used after a verb:*

> **Some** is used in affirmative sentences: There is *some* gasoline in the tank. **Any** is used in negative sentences: There is *not any* gasoline in the tank. Either **some** or **any** may be used in interrogative sentences, although **any** is much more frequently used in this case: Is there *any* gasoline in the tank?

---

*In oral answers, and in informal written work, you may practice the verbal contractions: is not—isn't, are not—aren't.

†Nouns which normally do not have a plural form are called "uncountable nouns."

Exercise B.

coffee	_____	bread	_____
coffeepot	_____	flower	_____
sugar	_____	refrigerator*	_____
milk	_____	library	_____

Answer "Yes" to the following questions:

1. Is there any coffee in the coffeepot?

   Yes, there is *some* coffee in the coffeepot.

2. Is there any milk in the refrigerator?

   Yes, _____.

3. Are there any flowers on the table?

   Yes, there are *some* _____.

4. Are there any children in the class?

   Yes, _____.

5. Is there any news on the radio?

   Yes, _____.

6. Are there any people in the library?

   Yes, _____.

Using Form 3, answer "No" to the same questions:

No, there isn't any coffee in the coffeepot.

No, _____.

No, there aren't any flowers on the table.

No, _____.

No, _____.

No, _____.

Dialog

Is there any news on television tonight?
Yes, there is some news on TV.
Is the news good or bad?
The news is good. The people are ready to vote.

*A refrigerator is sometimes called an "icebox."

LESSON VI

*Possessive Nouns and Possessive Adjectives
—whose as Interrogative—this, that, these,
those—come, go, get up, go to bed*

Look up **whose** (interrogative) in your dictionary. It asks a question about possession or ownership.

Whose book is this?
Who is the owner of this book?

Look up these words in your dictionary:

this _____	purse	_____
these _____	pocketbook	_____
	gloves	_____
that _____	coat	_____
those _____	newspaper	_____
	apartment	_____

POSSESSIVE NOUN		POSSESSIVE ADJECTIVE
	John has a car.	
It is *John's* car.		It is *his* car.
	Betty has friends.	
They are *Betty's* friends.		They are *her* friends.

21

Mrs. Brown has a
purse.

It is *Mrs. Brown's*
purse.

It is *her* purse.

My brother has an
apartment.

It is *my brother's*
apartment.

It is *his* apartment.

Mr. and Mrs.
Brown have a house.

It is *Mr. and Mrs.
Brown's* house.

It is *their* house.

Exercise A. Write the answers to the following questions, first with possessive nouns, then with possessive adjectives, as in the examples above.

1. Whose book is
   this? (Harold)

It is *Harold's* book.

It is *his* book.

2. Whose books
   are these?
   (Betty)

They are _____ .

They are ____ books.

3. Whose tickets
   are these?
   (Robert)

They _____ .

_____ .

4. Whose car is
   that? (my sister)

It _____ .

_____ .

5. Whose news-
   paper is this?
   (Mr. Brown)

_____ .

_____ .

6. Whose coat is
   this? (Miss
   Taylor)

_____ .

_____ .

7. Whose child is
   that? (my
   brother)

(It, He, or She) ____ .

_____ .

22

8. Whose children are those? (Mr. and Mrs. Brown)

_____.

_____.

9. Whose gloves are these? (Betty)

_____.

_____.

10. Whose house is this? (the doctor)

_____.

_____.

11. Whose purse is this? (the secretary)

_____.

_____.

Exercise B. Write the following definitions, and then answer "Yes" to the questions:

come _____   get up _____   early _____

go _____   go to bed _____   late _____

1. Do you go to bed early?   Yes, I _____.

2. Does Henry get up late?   Yes, he *gets* _____.

3. Does Betty get up early?   Yes, _____.

4. Do you and your brother come to school early?   Yes, we _____.

5. Do John and Alice come to school late?   Yes, _____.

Using Form 3 of the verb, answer "No" to the same questions:

No, I do not go _____.

No, he *does* not get _____.

No, she _____.

No, _____.

No, _____.

For Oral Drill, repeat all questions and answers many times, until your speech is *automatic*.

Dialog

Whose purse is this?
It is Betty's purse.
Are these her gloves, too?
No, those are not her gloves. They are Mrs. Brown's.

LESSON VII

*Prepositions **in, on,** and **at**—**sell** and **buy** —Buying and Selling Commodities in Common Use—Impersonal **you** and **they***

In is used with the name of a country, state, city, section of a city, mountains (plural), year, and month:

in Argentina	in the Rocky Mountains
in Texas	in the Andes
in New Orleans	in 1963
in the French Quarter	in January

On is used with the name of a street, avenue, ocean (or coast), river, lake, mountain (singular), day, and date:

on Clark Street	on the Ohio River
on Fifth Avenue	on Lake Superior
on the Pacific Ocean	on Mount Everest
on the Atlantic Coast	on Friday
on the Gulf of Mexico	on July 14
on Chesapeake Bay	on the 14th of July

At is used with an *exact* or restricted location, such as an airport, station, building, hotel, theater,* etc.; with an *exact* address; and with an *exact* hour.

at Kennedy Airport	at 343 Lexington Avenue
at Penn Station	at Broadway and 34th Street
at the Empire State	
Building	at 5:30 P.M.
at the Hilton Hotel	at noon, at midnight

*If you mean "inside" or "within," use the preposition **in.**

Special Uses

in the morning   *in* the afternoon   *in* the evening   *at* night

Exercise A.   Write the correct preposition (**in, on,** or **at**) in the question, and answer as indicated:

1. Does Henry live _____ Chicago?

   Yes, he _____.

2. Does he work _____ the airport?

   No, _____.

3. Does Alice live _____ Madison Street?

   Yes, _____.

4. Is the bank _____ Park Avenue?

   Yes, it _____.

5. Is St. Louis _____ Texas?

   No, it _____.

6. Is St. Louis _____ the Mississippi River?

   Yes, _____.

7. Is Chicago _____ Lake Michigan?

   Yes, _____.

8. Are Mr. and Mrs. Evans _____ the Statler Hotel?

   Yes, _____.

9. Is Lima _____ the Andes Mountains?

   Yes, _____.

10. Is Lima _____ Brazil?

    No, _____.

11. Is there a hotel _____ Lookout Mountain?

Yes, there _____.

12. Is John's birthday _____ September?

No, his birthday _____.

13. Do you go to school _____ Saturday?

No, _____.

14. Does Helen come to school _____ ten o'clock?

Yes, _____.

15. Is there a meeting _____ March 5?

Yes, there _____.

16. Does Frank live _____ 2122 Palm Street?

Yes, _____.

17. Is New York _____ the Pacific Coast?

No, _____.

18. Is Buenos Aires _____ the Caribbean Sea?

No, _____.

Exercise B. In this exercise, **when** and **where** are used to ask a question. Find these adverbs in your dictionary and distinguish carefully between them. Answer the questions in complete sentences, using **in, on,** or **at:**

1. Where do you live? _____.

2. Where does Harold live? _____.

3. Where is Miami? _____.

4. When does John get up? _____.

5. When do you go to bed? _____.

6. When is the meeting? _____.

7. Where is Mr. Brown now? _____.

8. Where is your house? _____.

9. Where is the hotel? _____.

10. When does John go to work? _____.

11. Where does he work? _____.

Sell and *Buy*—Buying and Selling Commodities

Exercise C. The verbs **sell** and **buy** follow the same pattern as **work** and **take**.

sell _____ buy _____

new _____ old _____ used (secondhand) ____

Answer "Yes" to the following questions:

1. Do you sell books?   Yes, _____.
2. Does Mr. Reed sell secondhand books?   Yes, _____.
3. Does Miss Mitchell sell
   flowers?   Yes, _____.
4. Do you and Ralph buy
   secondhand books?   Yes, _____.
5. Do the Taylor brothers buy
   used cars?   Yes, _____.

Using Form 3, answer "No" to the same questions:

No, I do not sell books.

No, he _____.

No, _____.

No, _____.

No, _____.

shoes _____ candy _____ clothing store _____

socks	_____	pencil	_____	drugstore	_____
stockings	_____	postcard	_____	grocery store	_____
suit	_____	stamp	_____	meat market	_____
soap	_____	toothpaste	_____	shoe store	_____

Impersonal *You* and *They*

In the following questions, **you** and **they** are used *impersonally— the pronouns do not refer to any specific person.* "Do you buy bread at the grocery store?" means "Does one buy bread at the grocery store?" "They don't sell stamps at the drugstore" means "Stamps are not sold at the drugstore." A question using the impersonal **you** retains the impersonal **you** in the answer.

> Example: Do you buy shoes at the shoe store? Yes, *you* buy shoes at the shoe store.
> Do they sell candy at the candy store? Yes, *they* sell candy at the candy store.

Exercise D. Answer the following questions:

1. Do you buy bread at the grocery store?

   Yes, you _____.

2. Where do you buy shoes?

   You _____.

3. Where do you buy postcards?

   _____.

4. Do they sell soap at the meat market?

   No, they _____.

5. Do they sell socks at the drugstore?

   No, _____.

6. Where do they sell socks?

   _____.

7. Do you buy candy at the clothing store?

   _____.

29

8. Where do they sell candy?

   _____ .

9. Where do you buy toothpaste?

   _____ .

10. Where do they sell stamps?

   _____ .

Dialog

Where is Mr. Brown's summer home?
It is on the Gulf Coast, near Tampa.
Is there a post office near his home?
No, there isn't any post office there. He buys his stamps at the store.

LESSON VIII

*Seasons of the Year—Days of the Week—
Expressions of Past Time—The Past Tense of
be, work, take, and **have***

The seasons of the year are winter, spring, summer, and fall
(autumn).
The days of the week are Sunday, Monday, Tuesday, Wednesday,
Thursday, Friday, and Saturday.

ago _____	morning _____	last night _____
show (*noun*) _____	afternoon _____	last week _____
meeting _____	evening _____	last month _____
at home _____	yesterday _____	last year _____
day before yesterday _____	night before last _____	

Past Tense of the Verb *Be**

FORM 1 AFFIRMATIVE	FORM 2 INTERROGATIVE	FORM 3 NEGATIVE
I was	was I?	I was not (I wasn't)
you were	were you?	you were not (you weren't)
he was, she was, it was	was he? was she? was it?	he was not, she was not, it was not
we were	were we?	we were not
you were	were you?	you were not
they were	were they?	they were not

*See also page 250, Appendix 1.

Exercise A.   Answer "Yes" to the following questions:

1. Were you busy yesterday?   Yes, _____.
2. Was Henry at home last
   night?   Yes, _____.
3. Was Alice at your house
   yesterday morning?   Yes, she was at my house _____.
4. Were you and your friends
   in New York last week?   Yes, we _____.
5. Were Mr. and Mrs. Allen at
   home last Sunday?   Yes, _____.

Using Form 3, answer "No" to the same questions:

No, I was not (wasn't) busy ____.

No, he _____.

No, _____.

No, _____.

No, _____.

Past Tense of the Verb *Work**

FORM 1	FORM 2	FORM 3
AFFIRMATIVE	INTERROGATIVE	NEGATIVE
I worked (one syllable)	did I work?†	I did not work (I didn't work)†
you worked	did you work?	you did not work
he worked, she worked, it worked	did he work? did she work? did it work?	he did not work, she did not work, it did not work
we worked	did we work?	we did not work
you worked	did you work?	you did not work
they worked	did they work?	they did not work

Exercise B.   Answer "Yes" to the following questions:

1. Did you work last week?   Yes, _____.
2. Did Frank work last Friday?   Yes, _____.

*See also page 254, Appendix 1.

†With the auxiliary **did,** the simple form of the verb (*the infinitive without to*) is used.

3. Did your sister work
   yesterday?   Yes, _____.
4. Did you and Tom work
   last night?   Yes, _____.
5. Did the boys work last
   Saturday?   Yes, _____.

Using Form 3, answer "No" to the same questions:

No, I did not (didn't) work _____.

No, he _____.

No, _____.

No, _____.

No, _____.

Past Tense of the Verb *Take*

Many of the most common English verbs are *irregular*, that is, they *do not form the past tense with "ed."* This irregularity is seen *only in Form 1* (affirmative) of the past tense. Forms 2 and 3 (interrogative and negative) are exactly similar to Forms 2 and 3 of the regular verbs, like **work**. In the next exercise, we will use the irregular verb **take**, whose past tense is *took*.

Exercise C. Answer "Yes" to the following questions:

1. Did you take aspirin last
   night?   Yes, I took _____.
2. Did Henry take Alice to the
   show the night before last?   Yes, he took _____.
3. Did Alice take English
   lessons last year?   Yes, _____.
4. Did you and your brother
   take Frank to the meeting
   last night?   Yes, we took _____.
5. Did Mr. and Mrs. Smith take
   their children to the show
   last Saturday?   Yes, _____.

Answer "No" to the same questions:

No, I did not take _____.

No, he did not take _____.

No, _____.

No, _____.

No, _____.

Past Tense of the Verb *Have*

The verb **have** is *irregular in the affirmative* (Form 1) of the past tense:

I had	we had
you had	you had
he had, she had, it had	they had

It is regular (like **work** and **take**) in the *interrogative* and *negative:*

(Form 2) did I have? (Form 3) I did not have

Exercise D. Answer "Yes" to the following questions:

1. Did you have your car last year? Yes, I had my car _____.
2. Did Mr. Taylor have his car last year? Yes, _____.
3. Did Mrs. Brown have her car six months ago? Yes, _____.
4. Did you and your sister have your car last spring? Yes, _____.
5. Did John and his brother have their car last summer? Yes, _____.

Using Form 3, answer "No" to the same questions:

No, I did not have _____.

No, he did not have _____.

No, _____.

No, _____.

No, _____.

Dialog

Did Mr. and Mrs. Lane have their car last year?
Yes, they had it last year.
Does Mrs. Lane take the children to school in the car?
Yes, she takes them to school every morning.

LESSON IX

*Past Tense of Regular and Irregular Verbs
—Adverbs of Frequency—Subject and Object
Pronouns—Possessive   Adjectives—"belong
to" with Pronoun Object*

Regular verbs form the past tense by adding "ed" to the simple form, that is, *the infinitive without to*:

> work—*worked*
> live—*lived**
> study—*studied**

Irregular verbs have *special past tense forms* in the affirmative (see Lesson VIII, pp. 33–34):

> take—*took*
> go—*went*
> come—*came*
> buy—*bought*
> sell—*sold*
> have—*had*

Adverbs of Frequency   (Footnotes 1 and 2 are in the box on p. 37.)

Some of the adverbs of frequency are:

always	_____	usually	_____
ever (at any time)[1]	_____	sometimes[2]	_____
never (at no time)	_____	often	_____

*For an explanation of *spelling changes*, see Lesson XXII, page 110.

Adverbs of frequency are placed *before the principal verb* (*not* the auxiliary):

> John *usually has* a class on Saturday.
> Helen does not *usually have* a class on Saturday.
> He *often studied* at night.
> She did not *often study* at night.
> Louis can *never be* here on Sunday.

Exception: When the verb is a form of **be** *with no auxiliary before it*, the adverb *follows the verb*:

> Louis *is never* here on Sunday.
> John *is often* here early.
> We *are usually* at home in the evening.

Exercise A.   The following questions are in pairs, or couples—*first the present tense*, and *then the past*.   Practice them carefully, remembering that the present tense auxiliary is **do** or **does**, while the past tense auxiliary is **did**.

1. Does Henry work at the post office? (present tense)

> Yes, he works _____ .

> No, he does not work _____ .
> Did he work there last summer? (past tense)

> Yes, he worked _____ .

> No, he did not work _____ .

---

[1] **Ever** is used *only in questions and negative sentences.*
In negative sentences, **not ever** usually changes to ***never***.
Example: Does John *ever* come early?
>   No, he *never* comes early. (No, he doesn't ever come early.)
Ever cannot be used in an affirmative sentence. If you answer "Yes," say:
>   Yes, he *often* comes early. Yes, he *sometimes* comes early.

[2] **Sometimes** cannot be used in a negative sentence.

2. Does Betty work on Saturday?

      Yes, _____.

      No, _____.

Did Helen work last Saturday?

      Yes, _____.

      No, _____.

3. Does Mary study at Franklin College?

      Yes, she studies _____.

      No, she _____.

Did she study English last year?

      Yes, _____.

      No, _____.

4. Do you always go home early?

      Yes, I always go _____.

      No, I do not always go _____.

Did you go home early last night?

      Yes, _____.

      No, _____.

5. Do you and John usually come to school on the bus?

      Yes, _____.

      No, we don't usually _____.

Did you (and John) come to school on the bus yesterday?

      Yes, _____.

      No, _____.

6. Does Mr. Russell sell used cars?

      Yes, he sells _____.

      No, _____.

Did he sell a car to Mr. Brown last month?

Yes, _____ .

No, _____ .

7. Do Mr. and Mrs. Dixon often buy flowers?

Yes, _____ .

No, _____ .

Did they buy any flowers the day before yesterday? (For the use of **some** and **any**, see Lesson V, p. 19.)

Yes, _____ .

No, _____ .

8. Does John always take Betty to school in his car?

Yes, _____ .

No, _____ .

Did he take her to school yesterday?

Yes, _____ .

No, _____ .

9. Do you ever eat lunch at home? (See examples of **ever**, p. 37.)

Yes, I sometimes _____ .

No, I never _____ .

Did you ever eat tacos when you were in Mexico?

Yes, I often ate _____ .

No, I never ate _____ .

Pronouns and Possessive Adjectives

Look up the verb **belong** in your dictionary. "Belong to" is followed by a noun or pronoun *object:*

The car belongs to *John*.

The car belongs to *Mr. and Mrs. Brown*.

The car belongs to *my brother and me*.

The car belongs to *him*.

The car belongs to *them*.

The car belongs to *us*.

Pronouns

SUBJECT	OBJECT	POSSESSIVE ADJECTIVE
I	me	my
you (singular)	you	your
he	him	his
she	her	her
it	it	its
we	us	our
you (plural)	you	your
they	them	their

Exercise B.

Fill in *pronoun object*:

1. The pen belongs to Ronald.   The pen belongs to ___. (him)
2. The gloves belong to Grace.   The gloves belong to ___.
3. The house belongs to my family (and me).   The house belongs to ___.
4. The car belongs to Mr. and Mrs. Brown.   The car belongs to ___.
5. The shoes belong to my brother.   The shoes belong to ___.

Fill in *possessive adjective:*

1a. It is Ronald's pen.   It is _____ pen. (his)
2a. They are Grace's gloves.   They are _____ gloves.
3a. It is my family's house.   It is _____ house.
4a. It is Mr. and Mrs. Brown's car.   It is _____ car.
5a. They are my brother's shoes.   They are _____ shoes.

Look up the following pronouns in your dictionary. Remember that in this lesson they are used *only with an interrogative meaning*:

SUBJECT	OBJECT	POSSESSIVE ADJECTIVE
who? _____	whom? _____	whose? _____

Exercise C: Oral practice. Answer the following questions, *using only the pronoun forms* used in Exercise B.

Whom does the dog belong to?
Whose dog is it?

Helen

Whom does the car belong to?
Whose car is it?

My family and I.

Whom do the flowers belong to?
Whose flowers are they?

Miss Taylor

Whom does the building belong to?
Whose building is it?

The Taylor brothers.

Whom does the bicycle belong to?
Whose bicycle is it?

Frank

Dialog

Do you usually go home early?
Yes, I do.
Did you go home early yesterday?
Yes, I went home very early yesterday.
Was your brother at home last night?
Yes, he was.

LESSON X

The Auxiliary Verb **can**—*Present and Past Tenses—Additional Prepositions—***how long? how far?**

The auxiliary verb **can** has *only two tenses, present* and *past.* In these two tenses, it follows *the same pattern* as the verb **be.** In other words, it *does not make use of the auxiliaries* **do, does,** and **did** in Forms 2, 3, and 4.

Note that in the present tense, 3d person singular, **can** *does not have* a final "s." As an auxiliary, can is *followed by the infinitive form* of the verb *without* **to.**

FORM 1	FORM 2	FORM 3
I can buy it.	Can I buy it?	I can not buy it.*
He can work.	Can he work?	He cannot work.*
They can go.	Can they go?	They can not go.

Present and Past Tenses

Write the definitions of these words in your own language, and learn their past tense forms:

PRESENT	PAST	PRESENT	PAST
can _____	could†	speak _____	spoke
eat _____	ate	stay _____	stayed

*****Can not** may also be written as one word: **cannot.** The contraction is **can't.**

†The pronunciation of **could** is similar to that of **good.**

Exercise A. Practice answering the following questions in present and past tenses:

1. Can John speak English now?

Yes, he can speak _____ .

No, he can not speak _____ .

Could David speak English last year?

Yes, he _____ .

No, he could not speak _____ .

2. Can you study this afternoon?

Yes, I _____ .

No, I _____ .

Could you study yesterday afternoon?

Yes, _____ .

No, _____ .

3. Is John here today?

Yes, _____ .

No, _____ .

Was he here yesterday?

Yes, _____ .

No, _____ .

4. Is there a meeting tonight? (For use of "there is," "there are," see Lesson V, p. 19.)

Yes, there is _____ .

No, there isn't _____ .

Was there a meeting last night?

Yes, _____ .

No, _____ .

5. Does Herbert live in Washington now?

Yes, _____ .

No, _____ .

Did he live in Washington six months ago?

Yes, _____ .

No, _____ .

6. Do Paul and Betty usually eat lunch at home?

Yes, _____.

No, _____.

Did they eat lunch at home last Tuesday?

Yes, _____.

No, _____.

Prepositions

Write the definitions in your own language. Note carefully the difference between *prepositions of time* and *prepositions of place*.

PLACE   TIME

in front of _____   near _____   before _____

behind _____   far from _____   after _____

as far as _____   until _____

next to _____

across from _____

The interrogative "how long?" (*relating to time*) may be answered in two ways:

How long did John stay at the office?

1 P.M. 2 P.M. 3 P.M. 4 P.M. 5 P.M.
————→ ———→ ———→ ———→

He stayed there *four hours*.
He stayed *until 5 p.m.*

The interrogative "how far?" (*relating to distance*) may be answered in two ways:

How far did you walk this morning?   I walked four blocks.

I walked as far as 10th Street.

Exercise B. Make one answer, either "Yes" or "No," to the following questions:

1. Does John live with his brother? _____.

2. Can you live without water? _____.
3. Do you go to school before 9:30? _____.

4. Do you study after dinner? _____.
5. Can Bob park his car in front of the store? _____.
6. Is the garage behind the house? _____.

7. Does Philip work until 5:30? _____.
8. Do you go as far as 10th Street on the bus? _____.
9. Is the school near your house? _____.
10. Is Cuba far from the coast of Florida? _____.
11. Is the drugstore next to the hospital? _____.
12. Is the doctor's office across from the hospital? _____.

Write definitions and study past tense forms:

birthday _____	VERBS	
block (city) _____	PRESENT TENSE	PAST
garden _____	park _____	parked
hour _____	put _____	put
vegetable _____	ride _____	rode
year _____	walk _____	walked

Exercise C. Give complete answer, using prepositions from this and previous lessons:

1. Where do you live? _____.

46

2. When is your birthday? _____.

3. Where does Henry work? _____.

4. Where is Chicago? _____.

5. Where is the hospital? _____.

6. Where is the doctor's office? _____.

7. Where does the doctor park his car? _____.

8. When is the meeting? _____.

9. When do you usually get up? _____.

10. Where is Mr. Brown's summer home? _____.

11. Where is Miami? _____.

12. Where is the flower garden? _____.
13. Where is the vegetable garden? _____.

14. Where is your money? _____.
15. How far do you ride on the bus? _____.

16. How long does Henry stay at the office? _____.

17. How long did Mr. Miller live in Miami? _____.

18. Can you work without a pencil? _____.

19. Whom do you live with? _____.

Dialog

Whom do the gloves belong to?
They belong to Miss Taylor.
And is this her purse?

No, it isn't. It's Betty's purse.
Did you buy the purse for Betty?
Yes, I bought it for her.

LESSON XI

*Future Tense—***much, many, a lot of, lots of,
how much? how many?***—Auxiliary Verbs* **can,
may,** *and* **must**—**must** *Replaced by* **have to**

Now you are ready to use three tenses: *present, past,* and *future.*
Study the future tense forms, pp. 250–251 and 255, Appendix 1.
Note that the auxiliary **will** is used for *all persons.* At one time, **shall**
was used instead of **will** in the first persons singular and plural, but
this usage is now rare.

Future Tense of the Verb *Have*

FORM 1 AFFIRMATIVE	FORM 2 INTERROGATIVE	FORM 3 NEGATIVE
I will have	will I have?	I will not have*
you will have	will you have?	you will not have
He will have,	will he have?	he will not have
she will have,	will she have?	she will not have,
it will have	will it have?	it will not have
we will have	will we have?	we will not have
you will have	will you have?	you will not have
they will have	will they have?	they will not have

Exercise A. Answer "Yes" to the following questions, which are in the
present, *past*, and *future tenses*:

1. Does Dick always take his money to the bank on Friday?

      Yes, he always takes _____ .

*The contraction of **will not** is "won't" (I *won't have*, etc.).

2. Did Helen take her money to the bank last week?

Yes, she took _____.

3. Will you take your money to the bank next week?

Yes, I will take _____.

Answer "No" to the same questions:

No, he does not _____.

No, she _____.

No, I _____.

Much, Many, etc.

much (*singular*) _____ Another way of saying **much** or **many**
                                    is **a lot of** or **lots of.**
many (*plural*) _____

    much money: a lot of money, lots of money.

    many friends: a lot of friends, lots of friends.

In English, we do not often use **much** with an affirmative verb.
We do not say: "He has much money," nor "I have much time."
Rather, we say: "He has *lots of money*," or "I have *a lot of time*."

Exercise B. Answer "Yes" to the following questions:

1. Do you have lots of time to study?

Yes, I have _____.

2. Did Olga have lots of friends in Costa Rica?

Yes, _____.

3. Will Henry have a lot of work to do next week?

Yes, _____.

Answer "No" to the same questions. Remember that it is all right to use
much with a *negative verb:*

No, I do not have _____.

No, she _____.

No, he _____.

To ask a question about quantity, use "how much?" or "how many?"

> *How much work* do you have to do?
> *How many classes* does Frank have today?

Exercise C.   Write questions (beginning with "How much _____"
or "How many _____") which correspond to the following statements:
(Remember that **much** is *singular* and **many** is *plural*.)

1. She has lots of work to do.

   How much work does she have to do?

2. I have three classes today.

   How many classes do you _____?

3. Helen has three sisters.

   _____?

4. Frank has $2,000 in the bank.

   _____?

5. They have one hour for lunch.

   _____?

6. The house has three doors.

   _____?

7. Mr. Allen bought five tickets.

   _____?

8. Mrs. Hill will buy four tickets.

   _____?

9. She had 50 cents in her purse.

   _____?

10. There is $1 in Charles's purse.

    How much money is there in Charles's purse?

11. There are nine boys in the class.

    _____?

12. There are six people in her family.

    _____?

Auxiliary Verbs *Can*, *May*, and *Must*

Review the auxiliary verb **can** in Lesson X, page 43. Two other auxiliary verbs are **may** and **must**. Remember that the interrogative and negative forms of the auxiliary verbs are *similar to those of the verb be* (they do not require **do** or **does** in these forms). Remember, too, that these verbs *do not add "s"* in the third person singular of the present affirmative.

Write the definitions of some new words:

drive _____ (past tense **drove**)   find _____ (past tense **found**)

leave _____ (past tense **left**)   job _____

Exercise D.

1. Can John speak French?

Yes, he _____ .   No, he _____ .

2. Can Helen drive a car?

Yes, _____ .   No, _____ .

3. Can you leave now?

Yes, _____ .   No, _____ .

The auxiliary verb **may** is similar to **can**:

He may go.   May he go?   He may not go.

However, the verb **may** has two different meanings. In the interrogative, *it asks permission to do something.* "May I go?" means "Do I have your permission to go?" In the affirmative and negative, *it indicates possibility in the future.* "I may go" means "Possibly I will go." "I may not go" means "Possibly I will not go."

Exercise E.   Answer the following questions, using **may** and **may not**:

1. Is it possible that you will go tomorrow?

I may go tomorrow.   I may not go tomorrow.

2. Is it possible that you will buy a car?

I _____ .   I may not _____ .

3. Is it possible that Henry will leave Monday?

He _____ .   He _____ .

52

The auxiliary verb **must** is *similar in form* to **can** and **may**.

We must go.   Must we go?   We must not go.

Must indicates a *strong obligation*, but it changes its meaning somewhat in the negative form. When we say "We must not go," we indicate that for some reason we are prohibited from going. Therefore, in Exercise F, we will use only Form 1 and Form 2, omitting the negative.

Exercise F.

1. Must you leave now?   Yes, I _____.
2. Must John take an
   examination this week?   Yes, _____.
3. Must Richard find a job?   Yes, _____.

Must **Replaced by** *Have to*

Another way of saying **must** is **have to**, *which can be used in the negative without any change in meaning.*

I must leave now.   —   I have to leave now.
Must he find a job?   —   Does he have to find a job?

Review the verb **have** in Lesson II, Lesson VIII, and the present lesson. **Have** is *not* similar to **can, may,** and **must** in the formation of the interrogative and negative. Follow your models of **have** in previous lessons.

Exercise G.   Answer "Yes" to the following questions:

1. Do Mr. and Mrs. Brown have
   to sell their house?   Yes, they have to _____.
2. Did John have to go home
   early last night?   Yes, he had to _____.
3. Will Alice have to stay at
   home tomorrow?   Yes, she will have to _____.

Answer "No" to the same questions (*present, past, and future*):

No, they do not have _____.

No, he _____.

No, she _____.

Answer "Yes":

4. Does Albert have to work
   until six?   Yes, he has to _____.

5. Did he have to work last
   Saturday?   Yes, _____.

6. Will he have to work next
   Saturday?   Yes, _____.

Using Form 3, answer "No" to the same questions:

No, he does not have _____.

No, he did not _____.

No, he will not _____.

Dialog

Does Frank study English at International House?

Yes, he studies English there at night.

Could he speak English six months ago?

No, he couldn't, but he speaks a lot now.

Can he park his car in front of International House during the class?

No, he can't park in front of the House, but he can park across the street.

LESSON XII

*Review of Sentence Structure in Present, Past, and Future Tenses—**must, have to**—City Locations with Prepositions and Prepositional Phrases—Distance in City Blocks*

downtown (*adverb*)	_____	PRESENT		PAST
out of town	_____	give	_____	gave
weekend	_____	move	_____	moved

Exercise A.   Answer "Yes" to the following questions:

PRESENT TENSE: 1. Does Miss Bradley give English lessons?

                       Yes, _____ .

PAST TENSE: 2. Did she give lessons last year?

                       Yes, _____ .

FUTURE TENSE: 3. Will she give lessons next summer?

                       Yes, _____ .

Using Form 3, answer "No" to the same questions:

                       No, she doesn't _____ .

                       No, _____ .

                       No, _____ .

Answer "Yes" to the following questions in the *present, past, and future:*

4. Do you have to eat downtown today?

    Yes, I _____ .

5. Did you have to eat downtown last night?

    Yes, I had _____ .

6. Will you have to eat downtown tomorrow night?

    Yes, _____ .

Using Form 3, answer "No" to the same questions:

    No, I do not _____ .

    No, I _____ .

    No, I _____ .

7. Must you move to a different apartment?

    Yes, I must _____ .
    (Do not answer in the negative. *See Lesson XI*, p. 53.)

8. Do you have to move next month?

    Yes, I have to _____ .

    No, I do not have to _____ .

City Locations

Study the city map shown opposite. Find all new words in your dictionary, and write them in your notebook.

Study the following prepositional forms *with the map:*

Where is the shoe store?

    It is *on* Washington Avenue *between* Fifth and Sixth Streets.
    It is *between* the department store and the hotel.
    It is *next to* the hotel.
    It is *across from* the Immigration Office.
    It is *around the corner from* the garage.

Where is the parking lot?

    It is *on the corner of* Washington Avenue and Fifth Street.

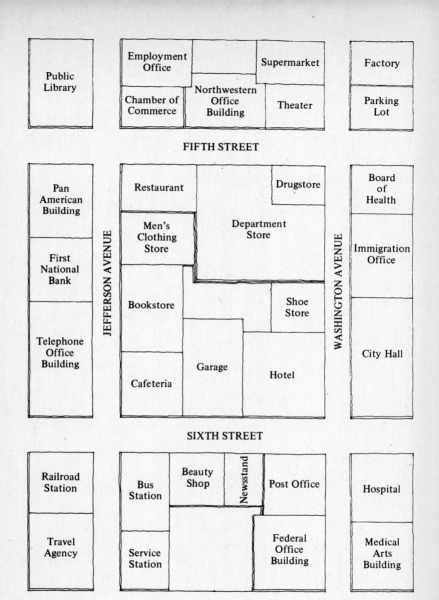

Public Library

Employment Office

Chamber of Commerce

Northwestern Office Building

Supermarket

Theater

Factory

Parking Lot

FIFTH STREET

Pan American Building

First National Bank

Telephone Office Building

JEFFERSON AVENUE

Restaurant

Men's Clothing Store

Bookstore

Cafeteria

Garage

Drugstore

Department Store

Shoe Store

Hotel

WASHINGTON AVENUE

Board of Health

Immigration Office

City Hall

SIXTH STREET

Railroad Station

Travel Agency

Bus Station

Beauty Shop

Newsstand

Post Office

Service Station

Federal Office Building

Hospital

Medical Arts Building

57

It is *next to* the factory.
It is *across from* the Board of Health.
It is *across from* the theater.
It is *catercorner* (diagonally) *across from* the
drugstore.

Exercise B. Using the *same prepositional forms*, fill in the answers to the
following questions:

1. Where is the Pan American Building?

    a. It is _____ Jefferson Avenue and Fifth Street.

    b. It is _____ the public library.

    c. It is _____ the First National Bank.

    d. It is _____ the restaurant.

    e. It is _____ the Chamber of Commerce.

2. Where is the garage?

    a. It is ____ Sixth Street ____ Washington and Jefferson Avenues.

    b. It is _____ the hotel and the cafeteria.

    c. It is _____ the hotel.

    d. It is _____ the beauty shop.

    e. It is _____ the bookstore.

3. Where is the Post Office?

    a. It is _____ Washington Avenue and Sixth Street.

    b. It is _____ the hotel.

    c. It is _____ the hospital.

    d. It is _____ the Federal Office Building.

    e. It is _____ the City Hall.

4. Where is the Northwestern Office Building?

    a. It is _____ Fifth Street _____ Washington and Jefferson Avenues.

    b. It is _____ the department store.

    c. It is _____ the Chamber of Commerce.

    d. It is _____ the Chamber of Commerce and the theater.

    e. It is _____ the supermarket.

Distance in City Blocks

In the city, we usually measure distance by *blocks*. For example:

The shoe store is *half a block from* the parking lot.
The cafeteria is *a block* (one block) *from* the City Hall.
The shoe store is *a block and a half from* the bus station.
The cafeteria is *two blocks from* the parking lot.
The supermarket is *two and a half blocks from* the railroad station.

Exercise C.

1. How far is the drugstore from the post office?

    It is _____ the post office.
2. How far is the garage from the City Hall?

    It is _____ the City Hall.
3. How far is the restaurant from the hospital?

    It is _____ the hospital.
4. How far is the newsstand from the restaurant?

    It is _____ the restaurant.
5. How far is the Medical Arts Building from the Public Library?

    It is _____ the Public Library.

Dialog

Where can I buy a newspaper?
You can buy a paper at the newsstand, across from the garage.
Where is the garage?
It's on Sixth Street, next to the hotel.
How far is it from the City Hall?
It's half a block from the City Hall.

LESSON XIII

Drill on Sentence Structure in Present, Past, and Future Tenses—Comparison of Adjectives—Adjectives Irregular in Comparison: **good, bad, much, many, little**

Exercise A.   Answer "Yes" to the following questions:

1. Does Miss Brown wear glasses?

   Yes, _____.

2. Did you wear your raincoat yesterday?

   Yes, I wore _____.

3. Will you wear your new shoes tomorrow?

   Yes, _____.*

Answer "No" to the same questions:

No, she does not _____.

No, _____.

No, _____.

(Review your study of **some** and **any**, Lesson V, p. 00.)

4. Do you have any extra paper?

   Yes, I _____.

*The contraction of "I will" is "I'll," *pronounced as one syllable.* *I'll, you'll, he'll, she'll, we'll, you'll,* and *they'll* are all pronounced as one syllable.   The 3d person singular *it'll* is pronounced in *two syllables.*   The contraction of "will not" is "won't"—see Lesson XI, page 49.

5. Did you buy any paper yesterday?

Yes, I _____ .

6. Will you bring some paper with you tomorrow?

Yes, I _____ .

Answer "No" to the same questions: (Use **any** with negative verb.)

No, I do not _____ .

No, I _____ .

No, I _____ .

Comparison of Adjectives

	COMPARATIVE	SUPERLATIVE
old _____	older _____	the oldest _____
young _____	younger _____	the youngest _____
tall _____	taller _____	the tallest _____
short _____	shorter _____	the shortest _____
easy _____	easier _____	the easiest _____
pretty _____	prettier _____	the prettiest _____
simple _____	simpler _____	the simplest _____

If the adjective has three or more syllables,* do not add "er" and "est" to form the comparative and superlative. Use the words *more* and *most* as shown below:

difficult ___ more difficult the most difficult

expensive ___ more expensive the most expensive

*Many two-syllable adjectives may form the comparative and superlative in either of the two ways, for example: *pleasant, pleasanter, the pleasantest*—or: *pleasant, more pleasant, the most pleasant.*

Irregular Comparisons:

good	_____	better	_____	the best	_____
bad	_____	worse	_____	the worst	_____
much†	_____	more	_____	the most	_____
many	_____	more	_____	the most	_____
little‡	_____	less	_____	the least	_____
few§	_____	fewer	_____	the fewest	_____

John
8 years old

Tom
11 years old

Helen
10 years old

Betty
15 years old

Frank
17 years old

as old as	_____	older than	_____	the oldest	_____
as young as	_____	younger than	_____	the youngest	_____
as tall as	_____	taller than	_____	the tallest	_____
as short as	_____	shorter than	_____	the shortest	_____

Exercise B.

1. Is Betty as tall as Frank? No, she is not as tall as Frank.
2. Is Betty taller than Helen? Yes, she is taller than Helen.

3. Is John as old as Tom? _____.

4. Is Frank taller than Betty? _____.

†Remember that **much** is *singular* and **many** is *plural*.

‡**Little** (in this comparison) refers to *quantity*, and *not to size*. For example: He has *little time* to study—or: He has *a small amount of* (not much) *time* to study.

§**Few** is *plural*, in contrast with **little**, which is *singular*. **Few** is regular in the comparative and superlative forms.

63

5. Is Helen as tall as Tom? _____.

6. Is Helen as tall as Betty? _____.

7. Is Tom as short as John? _____.

8. Is John younger than Tom? _____.

9. Is Betty as old as Frank? _____.

10. Is Helen older than John? _____.

11. Is Tom older than Helen? _____.

12. Is Tom as old as Betty? _____.

13. Is Tom younger than Frank? _____.

14. Is Betty the oldest? _____.

15. Is Helen the shortest? _____.

16. Is John the youngest? _____.

17. Who is the tallest? _____.

Dialog

Is Helen as old as Tom?
No, she is younger than Tom.
But she is as tall as he is.
Yes, but she isn't as tall as her sister Betty. Betty is much taller than Helen.

LESSON XIV

*Telling Time—Continuous Form of Pres-
ent Tense—Use of Present Simple and Present Continuous Forms—Comparison of Adjectives:* **old, new, long, short**

Continuous Form of Present Tense

FORM 5	FORM 6	FORM 7
I am eating	am I eating?	I am not eating
you are eating	are you eating?	you are not eating
he (she) is eating	is he (she) eating?	he (she) is not eating
we are eating	are we eating?	we are not eating
you are eating	are you eating?	you are not eating
they are eating	are they eating?	they are not eating

In Appendix 1, study the same forms, 5, 6, and 7, of the verb **work** (p. 254). These are the *continuous forms*. Compare them with the *simple forms* of the same tense: Forms 1, 2, and 3.

Exercise A. Change the following verbs from

FORM 1	TO	FORM 5		FORM 2	TO	FORM 6
I eat		I am eating		do I eat?		am I eating?
1. you work		you are working		1. do you speak?		are you _____?
2. he has		he is having		2. does he wear?		_____?
3. she takes		she _____		3. does she buy?		_____?
4. we sell		we _____		4. do we study?		_____?

Ten-ten.
Ten minutes past ten.
Ten minutes after ten.

Ten fifteen.
Fifteen minutes
past ten.
A quarter past ten.

Ten-thirty.
Half-past ten.

Ten-thirty-five.
Twenty-five
minutes to eleven.

Ten-forty-five.
A quarter to eleven.

Ten-fifty.
Ten minutes
to eleven.

What time is it?

It's (it is)
two o'clock.
_____
_____
_____

_____
_____
_____

Form 1	to	Form 5		Form 2	to	Form 6
5. you come		you _____		5. do you go?		_____?
6. they go		they _____		6. do they take?		_____?

Form 3   to   Form 7

I do not study   I am not studying

1. you do not eat   you are not _____

2. he does not take   _____

3. she does not come   _____

4. we do not have   _____

5. you do not speak   _____

6. they do not study   _____

Use of Present Simple and Present Continuous Forms

The *simple form* of the present tense describes an action which is *customary, frequent,* or *generally true:*

> Where does Mr. Taylor work?   He works at the bank.

The *continuous form* of the present tense describes an activity which is *taking place at the present time*—at this moment, today, this week, this month, or this year:

> Is Mr. Taylor working today?   No, he is not working today.

Exercise B.

Customary action: 1. Do Jane and Grace study every night?

Yes, they _____ .   No, they do not

_____ .

Present activity: 2. Are they studying now?

Yes, they are _____ .   No, they are not

_____ .

Continue questions and answers, using the simple or continuous forms of the present tense as required:

3. Does Betty usually wear a hat?

Yes, _____ .   No, _____ .

4. Is she wearing a hat today?

Yes, _____ .   No, _____ .

5. Do the Browns always have dinner at 6:30?

Yes, they _____ .   No, _____ .

6. Are they having dinner now?

Yes, _____ .   No, _____ .

7. Does Henry study a lot?

Yes, _____ .   No, _____ .

8. Is he studying chemistry this year?

Yes, _____ .   No, _____ .

Comparison of Adjectives

These are Helen's dresses. She bought:

| the white dress yesterday. | the blue dress two years ago. | the striped dress last year. | the green dress last month. |

The white one.   The blue one.   The green one.

The striped one.

as old as _____	older than _____	the oldest _____
as new as _____	newer than _____	the newest _____
as long as _____	longer than _____	the longest _____
as short as _____	shorter than _____	the shortest _____

Exercise C.   Refer to the illustration on p. 68.

1. Is the striped dress longer than the blue one? _____.
2. Is the white dress newer than the green one? _____.
3. Is the blue dress as long as the white one? _____.
4. Is the striped dress as old as the blue one? _____.
5. Is the blue dress older than the white one? _____.
6. Is the white dress as short as the blue one? _____.
7. Is the green dress longer than the white one? _____.
8. Is the striped dress newer than the blue one? _____.
9. Is the white dress shorter than the green one? _____.
10. Is the blue dress as new as the green one? _____.
11. Is the white dress as old as the striped one? _____.
12. Is the green dress older than the white one? _____.

Dialog

Can you tell me what time it is?
I can't see my watch without my glasses, but I think it's about half-past three.
Don't you usually wear glasses?
Yes, but I am not wearing them today.

LESSON XV

Review of Telling Time—Review of Sentence Structure in Present (Simple and Continuous Forms), Past, and Future Tenses—Adverbs, Regular and Irregular—Comparative Form of Adverbs

Exercise A.

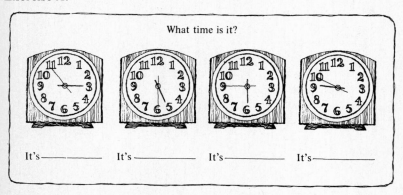

What time is it?

It's ———   It's ———   It's ———   It's ———

Review of Sentence Structure in Present, Past, and Future Tenses

In the following questions and answers, we may practice using the contractions of auxiliary verbs. Contractions for the future tense are in the footnote on page 61. Remember that *we do not usually write contractions*—we use them in conversation and *informal* letters.

rain (*noun*) ——————   To "take a nap" means to "sleep for a short time."

rain (*verb*) ——————   *Children often "take a nap" in the afternoon.*

Exercise B.

Present Tense (simple)

Yes, he takes _____ .

1. Does Johnny take a nap every day?

No, he doesn't take

_____ .

Present Tense (continuous)
Yes, he's taking*

_____ .

2. Is he taking a nap now?

No, he isn't taking

_____ .

Past Tense (simple)

Yes, he took _____ .

3. Did he take a nap yesterday?

No, he didn't take

_____ .

Future Tense (simple)
Yes, he'll take _____ .

4. Will he take a nap tomorrow?

No, he won't take

_____ .

5. Does your cousin work at the library?

Yes, _____ .

No, _____ .

6. Is he working today?

Yes, _____ .

No, _____ .

7. Did he work last Saturday?

Yes, _____ .

No, _____ .

8. Will he work tomorrow night?

Yes, _____ .

No, _____ .

*In the 3d person singular, the contractions *he's*, *she's*, and *it's* may be used instead of *he is*, *she is*, and *it is*. Distinguish carefully between "it's" (contraction of *it is*) and "its" (possessive).

9. Does it usually
rain in
November?

Yes, it usually rains
_____ .

No, it _____ .

10. Is it raining
now?

Yes, _____ .

No, _____ .

11. Did it rain
last night?

Yes, it rained _____ .

No, _____ .

12. Will it rain
tomorrow?

Yes, _____ .

No, _____ .

13. Do Mr. and
Mrs. Spencer
often have
guests?

Yes, they _____ .

No, _____ .

14. Are they having
guests this
week?

Yes, _____ .

No, _____ .

15. Did they have
guests last
week?

Yes, _____ .

No, _____ .

16. Will they have
guests next
summer?

Yes, _____ .

No, _____ .

Adverbs, Regular and Irregular

Regular adverbs are formed by adding "ly" to the adjective:

ADJECTIVE	ADVERB	ADJECTIVE	ADVERB
bad	_____ badly	quick	_____ quickly

72

ADJECTIVE	ADVERB	ADJECTIVE	ADVERB
honest	_____ honestly	rapid	_____ rapidly
loud	_____ loudly*	slow	_____ slowly
nice	_____ nicely	soft	_____ softly
		sweet	_____ sweetly

	IRREGULAR
ADJECTIVE	ADVERB
good _____ well
fast _____ fast
hard _____ hard

("Hard" in this case means *strenuously* or *with difficulty*.)

Exercise C.   Write definitions for these new words. Note that several of the words may be either *noun* or *verb*.

business_____   cook (*noun*) _____

clothes _____   cook (*verb*) _____

merchant _____   dress (*noun*) _____

run _____   dress (*verb*) _____

sing _____   shout (*noun*) _____

travel _____   shout (*verb*) _____

voice_____

Fill in the blanks with the *corresponding adverb:*

Adjective	*Adverb*
1. The train is *slow*.	The train runs ____(slowly)____ .
2. Helen wears *nice* clothes.	Helen dresses _____ .
3. She gave me a *quick* answer.	She answered me _____ .

*"Loud" may also be used as an adverb.

ADJECTIVE	ADVERB
4. Tom's writing is *bad*.	Tom writes _____.
5. Helen has a *sweet* voice.	Helen sings _____.
6. Mr. Ellis is an *honest* merchant.	Mr. Ellis does business _____.
7. We traveled on a *fast* plane.	We traveled _____.
8. Mrs. Peterson is a *good* cook.	Mrs. Peterson cooks _____.
9. John gave a *loud* shout.	John shouted _____.
10. Barbara has a *soft* voice.	Barbara speaks _____.
11. Henry's work is *hard*.	Henry works _____.

Comparative Form of Adverbs

REGULAR		IRREGULAR	
slowly	more slowly than	well, nicely	better than
quickly	more quickly than	fast	faster than
softly	more softly than	badly	worse than
sweetly	more sweetly than	hard (strenuously)	harder than

Exercise D. Fill in the blanks with a *comparative* adverbial phrase:

1. The train travels ___*(more slowly than)*___ the plane.

2. Helen speaks _____ John.

3. Mrs. Peterson cooks _____ her sister.

4. Betty answered the question _____ Philip.

5. The plane travels _____ the boat.

6. Albert writes _____ Tom.

7. My brother works _____ I.

8. Grace sings _____ Helen.

9. Helen dresses _____ Grace.

Dialog

Did you take the bus to Nashville?
No, we took the train because it goes faster than the bus.
If you could take an express bus, it goes almost as fast as the train.
Yes, but most of the buses are local, and they travel more slowly
than the train.

LESSON XVI

Review of Verbal Contractions—Drill on Sentence Structure in Present, Past, and Future Tenses—Verbs Requiring Preposition before Direct Object: **look at, listen to, wait for**—*Review of Comparative Form of Adverbs—Possessive Pronouns*

Remember to practice the contractions orally:

are not	... aren't (1 syllable)	do not	... don't (1 syllable)
is not	... isn't (2 syllables)	does not	... doesn't (2 syllables)
was not	... wasn't (2 syllables)	did not	... didn't (2 syllables)
were not	... weren't (1 syllable)	will not	... won't (1 syllable)

New Words:

PRESENT   PAST

listen _____ listened (2 syllables)   program _____

look _____ looked (1 syllable)   news program _____

wait _____ waited (2 syllables)   report _____

write _____ wrote   weather report _____

Exercise A. Answer "Yes" to the following questions:

Present Simple

1. Does Mr. Davis write the report every month?   Yes, he writes _____.

Present Continuous

2. Is he writing the report now?   Yes, he is writing _____.

Past

3. Did he write the report last
   month?

Yes, he _____.

Future

4. Will he write the report next
   month?

Yes, he _____.

Answer "No" to the same questions:

No, he does not write _____.

No, he _____.

No, he _____.

No, he _____.

Verbs Requiring Preposition before Direct Object

Some verbs require a preposition before a direct object. The most commonly used are:

look *at* _____   listen *to* _____   wait *for* _____

Exercise B.   *Look at.* Answer "Yes" to the following questions:

1. Do the children look *at* television every night?

   Yes, they _____.

2. Are they looking at television now?

   Yes, _____.

3. Did you look at the weather report yesterday?

   Yes, I looked _____.

4. Will you look at the weather report tomorrow?

   Yes, I _____.

Answer "No" to the same questions:

No, they do not _____.

No, they are not _____.

No, I _____.

No, _____.

Listen to.   Answer "Yes" to these questions:
5. Does John always listen *to* the news program?

Yes, he always _____.
6. Is he listening to the news program now?

Yes, _____.
7. Did you listen to the music last night?

Yes, I _____.
8. Will you listen to the program tomorrow night?

Yes, _____.

Answer "No" to the same questions:

No, he doesn't always listen _____.

No, he isn't _____.

No, I didn't _____.

No, I won't _____.

Wait for.   Answer "Yes":
9. Does Frank usually wait *for* Alice?

Yes, _____.
10. Is he waiting for the bus now?

Yes, _____.
11. Did you wait for him last night?

Yes, _____.
12. Will you wait for Alice until 8 o'clock?

Yes, _____.

Answer "No" to the same questions:

No, _____.

No, _____ .

No, I _____ .

No, _____ .

Exercise C.   Review the Comparative Form of Adverbs. Answer "Yes" or "No" to the following questions, as indicated:

1. Does Tom drive more slowly than Henry?

Yes, _____ .

2. Does Grace answer more quickly than Helen?

Yes, _____ .

3. Does Helen cook better than Grace?

Yes, _____ .

4. Does the bus travel faster than the train?

No, _____ .

5. Does Frank work harder than you?

No, _____ .

6. Does Frank work more slowly than George?

Yes, _____ .

Possessive Pronouns

Consult your dictionary and write the meaning of each pronoun:

mine _____   ours   _____

yours _____   yours (*plural*) _____

his _____   theirs   _____

hers _____

The possessive pronoun is *never followed by a noun*. Compare it with the possessive *adjective* (Lesson VI) which is *always followed by a noun*.

Exercise D.   Change from possessive adjective to possessive pronoun:

POSSESSIVE ADJECTIVE | POSSESSIVE PRONOUN
1. It is *my* book. | The book is *mine*.

2. They are my gloves. The gloves are _____ .

3. It is our car. The car is _____ .

4. It is his watch. The watch is _____ .

5. They are her magazines. The magazines are _____ .

6. It is your ticket. The ticket is _____ .

7. It is their house. The house is _____ .

Review the use of "belong to" in Lesson IX. Then change to possessive pronoun:

OBJECT PRONOUN	POSSESSIVE PRONOUN
8. The money belongs to her.	The money is _____ .
9. The car belongs to me.	The car is _____ .
10. The tickets belong to them.	The tickets are _____ .
11. The gloves belong to you.	The gloves are _____ .
12. The house belongs to us.	The house is _____ .
13. The furniture belongs to him.	The furniture is _____ .

Change from the possessive pronoun to the object pronoun:

POSSESSIVE PRONOUN	OBJECT PRONOUN
14. The tickets are mine.	The tickets belong to __(me)__ .
15. The car is theirs.	The car belongs to _____ .
16. The gloves are hers.	The gloves belong to _____ .
17. The radio is his.	The radio belongs to _____ .
18. The furniture is yours.	The furniture belongs to _____ .
19. The dog is ours.	The dog belongs to _____ .

80

Oral Practice:

Whose money is it?
Whom does the money belong to?

Whose car is it?
Whom does the car belong to?

Whose house is it?
Whom does the house belong to?

Whose suitcase is it?
Whom does it belong to?

Whose books are they?
Whom do the books belong to?

Whose children are they?
Whom do they belong to?

Dialog

Are the boys looking at TV now?
No, they're listening to the radio. They're waiting for the news program.
Does the radio belong to them?
Yes, it's theirs. The TV set isn't theirs—it's mine.

LESSON XVII

*Sentence Structure Drill—Future Expressed by **"going to"** plus Verb—Review of Possessive Nouns and Pronouns, with Comparative Forms of **large, big, and small***

give _____   rent _____   party _____

marry* _____   visit (verb) _____   vacation _____

Exercise A.

1. Does Mrs. Adams often give parties?

    Yes, _____.
2. Is she giving a party today?

    Yes, _____.
3. Did she give a party the night before last?

    Yes, _____.
4. Will she give a party tomorrow night?

    Yes, _____.

Answer "No" to the same questions:

No, she does not _____.

No, she _____.

*The verb **marry**, when it does not have an object, is usually expressed idiomatically as "get married."

No, _____.

No, _____.

Future Expressed by "*Going to*" plus Verb

Exercise B. Write the verb **go** in the present continuous form (Form 5):

I am going   She _____

You _____   We _____

He _____   They _____

When we add the infinitive to the continuous form of **go** we indicate that the action will occur in the future.

> I am going to buy a car next week—I will buy a car next week.
>
> John is going to stay with me tomorrow—John will stay with me tomorrow.

Change the following sentences by using "going to" in place of **will:**
> I will bring my sister with me tomorrow night.
> I am going to bring my sister with me tomorrow night.

1. John will rent the apartment next month.

   John is going _____.
2. Mrs. Adams will give a party Friday night.

   Mrs. Adams _____.
3. We will sell our house.

   We _____.
4. They will take their vacation in October.

   They _____.

Use "going to" in your answers to the following questions:

5. Is Henry going to buy a car next month?

   Yes, he _____.
6. Are you going to pay for the tickets?

   Yes, I _____.

7. Is Alice going to get married next summer?

Yes, she _____.

8. Are we going to stay here?

Yes, _____.

9. Are Mr. and Mrs. Smith going to rent the apartment?

Yes, they _____.

Answer "No" to the same questions:

No, he is not going to _____.

No, I _____.

No, she _____.

No, we _____.

No, they _____.

Exercise C. Answer the following questions, adding a phrase which denotes some time in the future, e.g., "tomorrow night," "next year," etc.

1. When are you going to buy the book?

I _____ (tomorrow) _____.

2. When is John going to get married?

He _____.

3. When is Helen going to take the examination?

She _____.

4. When are we going to pay for the tickets?

We _____.

5. When are Mr. and Mrs. Thomas going to visit us?

They _____.

Repeat many times in oral practice.

84

Review of Possessive Nouns and Pronouns

Exercise D.

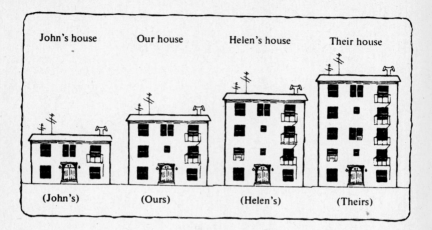

as large as _____ larger than _____ the largest _____

as big as _____ bigger than _____ the biggest _____

as small as _____ smaller than _____ the smallest _____

1. Is Helen's house bigger than John's? _____.
2. Is our house smaller than theirs? _____.
3. Is John's house as big as Helen's? _____.
4. Is our house as big as Helen's? _____.
5. Is their house as small as ours? _____.

6. Which house is the smallest? _____.

7. Is Helen's house the biggest? _____.

Dialog

I'm going to show you a picture of my house. (showing picture)
It's a very nice house, much bigger than ours.

Thank you, but I'm sure it isn't as nice as yours.
When are you going to visit us?
I hope I can visit you next summer.

LESSON XVIII

Bring and take, with Drill on Verb Tenses—Review of going to—Future Expressed by Present Continuous Form—much, more, most; and little, less, least

The verb **take** has several different meanings. (See Lesson II, p. 6.) One of its meanings is "to carry or convey to *another place* (away from the speaker)":

I am going to *take* this book home with me.

In this sense, we can say that **bring** is the *opposite of take*, because **bring** means "to carry or convey *to this place* (the place of the speaker)":

I am going to *bring* the book to this class.

Find these two words in your dictionary, and learn their past tense forms:

bring _____   past tense: **brought**

take _____   past tense: **took**

Write the definitions of these four new words:

cleaner (*noun*) _____   notebook _____

home _____   suit (*noun*) _____

Exercise A. When you answer the following questions, use the pronoun object indicated with the question:

1. Do you always bring your notebook to this class?

   <u>it</u>

   Yes, I always bring it to this class.
2. Did Helen bring her brother to this class yesterday?

   <u>him</u>

   Yes, _____ .
3. Will you bring Margaret with you tomorrow?

   <u>her</u>

   Yes, _____ .
4. Are you going to bring Margaret with you tomorrow?

   Yes, _____ .

Using Form 2, answer "No" to the same questions:

   No, I do not always _____ .

   No, she did not _____ .

   No, I will not _____ .

   No, I am not going to _____ .

Using the verb **take,** answer "Yes" to the following questions:

5. Does Mrs. Brown take the children to school every day?

   <u>them</u>

   Yes, _____ .
6. Did you take your suit to the cleaner's last week?

   <u>it</u>

   Yes, _____ .

7. Will John take the books home with him?

them

    Yes, _____ .

8. Is John going to take the books home with him?

    Yes, _____ .

Answer "No" to the same questions:

    No, she does not take _____ .

    No, I _____ .

    No, he _____ .

    No, he _____ .

arrive _____ come back (return here) _____

leave _____ go back (return there) _____

Future Expressed by Present Continuous Form

Review Lesson XVII with "going to" used to express future time. In the United States, it is becoming more and more common to hear the *present continuous form* of the verb used to indicate future time, without "will" and without "going to." This is especially true of the verbs **go**, **come**, **leave**, and **arrive**, although the practice is not limited to these verbs. For example:

> They are moving to another apartment next month.
> John and Mary are getting married next summer.

Since this practice is *not applicable to all verbs*, it is not advisable for the beginner to adopt it. He must, however, be able to understand when he sees or hears it. In the case of the four verbs (**go**, **come**, **leave**, **arrive**) the practice is completely accepted.

In the following examples, *all three forms in each group have the same meaning*, and indicate future time:

> $\begin{cases} \text{I will go to Chicago next week.} \\ \text{I am going to go to Chicago next week.} \\ \text{I am going to Chicago next week.} \end{cases}$

> They will leave tomorrow.
> They are going to leave tomorrow.
> They are leaving tomorrow.

> He will come the day after tomorrow.
> He is going to come the day after tomorrow.
> He is coming the day after tomorrow.

> She will arrive next Monday.
> She is going to arrive next Monday.
> She is arriving next Monday.

Exercise B. The following future-time sentences may be written in *three* different ways, like the sentences above. In each group, supply the *other two* forms:

1. Helen will come back next month.

   Helen is going to _____.

   Helen is coming _____.

2. Ralph is going to go to Chicago soon.

   Ralph _____.

   Ralph _____.

3. I am going back to work tomorrow.

   I _____.

   I _____.

4. They are arriving tomorrow night.

   They will _____.

   They are going to _____.

5. We will leave before Christmas.

   We _____.

   We _____.

6. Tom is going to come to school with me.

   Tom _____.

   Tom _____.

Oral Practice:

What are you going to do tomorrow night?

I _____.

What are you going to do next weekend?

I _____.

90

Much, More, Most and Little, Less, Least

The black hat. The pink hat. The red hat. The green hat.

The black one. The pink one. The red one. The green one.
$3.98 $7.50 $9.95 $7.50

Exercise C.

cost (*verb*) _____ black _____ pink _____ red _____ green _____

blue _____ brown _____ dark _____ light _____

as much as _____ more than _____ the most _____

as little as _____ less than _____ the least _____

1. Does the pink hat cost more than the black one?

   Yes, the pink hat costs _____.

2. Does the black hat cost as much as the green one?

   No, it doesn't cost _____.

3. Does the pink hat cost less than the red one?

   _____.

4. Does the green hat cost as much as the pink one?

   _____.

5. Does the black hat cost less than the pink one?

   _____.

6. Does the green hat cost as much as the red one?

   _____.

7. Does the red hat cost more than the pink one?

   _____.

8. Which hat costs the least?

_____.

9. Which hat costs the most?

_____.

Dialog

I'm going to buy a new hat, but I can't make up my mind which
   one to buy.

I like the green one. It is pretty, and it costs less than the red one.

I like the red one better, even if it costs the most.

I think the black one is pretty, too, and it doesn't cost as much as
   the others.

LESSON XIX

Want and like—enjoy Followed by ING-form of Verb—Review of Prepositions with Pronoun Objects—Very and Too

Look up these verbs in your dictionary, and distinguish carefully between them:

want _____ like _____

Want means *to desire*. **Like** means *to enjoy*. These verbs are regular, and their past tenses are **wanted** (two syllables) and **liked** (one syllable).

dance _____ talk _____ concert _____

downtown (*adverb*) _____ package _____

Exercise A.

1. Do you like coffee?

Yes, _____. No, _____.

2. Do you want a cup of coffee?

Yes, _____. No, _____.

3. Does Henry like music?

Yes, _____. No, _____.

4. Does he want a ticket for the concert?

Yes, _____. No, _____.

5. Did you like the
   concert last
   night?

Yes, _____.   No, _____.

Exercise B.   The verbs **want** and **like** may be followed by another verb
in the infinitive form:

1. Do you like to
   eat downtown?

Yes, _____.   No, _____.

2. Do you want to
   eat downtown
   tonight?

Yes, _____.   No, _____.

3. Does Henry like
   to dance?

Yes, _____.   No, _____.

4. Does he want to
   go to the dance
   with us?

Yes, _____.   No, _____.

5. Did Mr. Adams
   like to dance
   when he was
   young?

Yes, _____.   No, _____.

Enjoy Followed by ING-form of Verb

Exercise C.   **Enjoy** has the same meaning as **like**, but it is followed by the
ING-form of the verb, and *never by an infinitive:*

1. Do you enjoy
   television?

Yes, _____.   No, _____.

2. Do you enjoy
   watching
   television?

Yes, _____.   No, _____.

3. Does Henry
   enjoy dancing?

Yes, _____.   No, _____.

4. Did he enjoy the
party last night?

Yes, _____ .   No, _____ .

5. Did you enjoy
talking with
Betty?

Yes, _____ .   No, _____ .

Review of Prepositions with Pronoun Objects

Review prepositions:

on	for	between	in front of	before
in	from	with	behind	after
at	to	without	next to	until

Pronoun objects of prepositions:

me   you   him   her   it   one   us   them

If a noun has a *definite article* (*the* house), the *corresponding pronoun is* **it.**

Did you buy the house?   Yes, we bought it.

If a noun has an *indefinite article* (*a* house), the *corresponding pronoun is* **one.**

Did you buy a house?   Yes, we bought one.

Exercise D.   Write the correct object pronoun in the blank space:

1. The package is for _____ .
(my brother)

2. He sent the telegram to _____ .
(Margaret)

3. We bought the flowers for _____ .
(my aunt)

4. We spoke to _____ .
(Mr. and Mrs. Jones)

5. The letter is from _____ .
(my father)

6. I can't go without _____ .
(my sister)

7. John paid for _____ .
(the ticket)

8. Grace paid for _____ , too.
(a ticket)

9. Bob sat in front of _____ .
(my brother and me)

10. We sat behind _____ .
(Bob and Helen)

11. Olga sat between _____ .
(Frank and his sister)

12. There isn't any sugar in _____ .
(the coffee)

13. We went downtown with _____ .
(the lawyer)

14. They won't go without _____ .
(me and my friends)

15. We looked at _____ yesterday.
(an apartment)

16. We didn't rent _____ .
(the apartment)

Special care must be exercised with an object composed of two pronouns (*her* and *me*) or of a noun and a pronoun (*Betty* and *him*). Some people might say, "He bought the tickets for John and I." *This is not correct.* You must say, "He bought the tickets for John and me," because **me** is the *object of a preposition*.

Study the following examples:

He speaks French with *her and me*.	(*not* she and I)
They came with *Helen and me*.	(*not* Helen and I)
The work was done by *him and his brother*.	(*not* he and his brother)
All of *us students* went to the meeting.	(*not* we students)
This notice is for *us and them*.	(*not* we and they)

Choose the correct pronoun and write it in the blank space:

17. Mr. Miller got tickets for _____ and John.
$\qquad$ (he, him)

18. He gave the flowers to _____ and _____.
$\qquad$ (she, her) $\qquad$ (I, me)

19. John sat between Helen and _____ .
$\qquad$ (I, me)

20. Many of _____ Cubans came to the United States.
$\qquad$ (we, us)

21. We came with _____ and his wife.
$\qquad$ (he, him)

The same care must be exercised with pronoun objects of a verb:

> I saw *him* and Mr. John-
> son downtown. (*not* he and Mr. Johnson)
> She told John and *me* to
> come early. (*not* John and I)

Very and Too

Care must be taken to distinguish between the adverbs **very** and **too.**

Used before an adjective or adverb **very** means *extremely* and **too** means *excessively.*

EXTREMELY	EXCESSIVELY (TO AN UNDESIRABLE DEGREE)
Helen is *very* tired.	She is *too* tired to go the party.
Johnny is *very* young.	He is *too* young to go to school.
Ray speaks *very* fast.	I can't understand Ray because he speaks *too* fast.

Exercise E. Fill in the blanks with **very** or **too**, according to the meaning of the sentence:

1. Your new hat is _____ pretty.

2. Our trip was _____ pleasant.

3. I can't go to the show because I am _____ tired to go out.

4. Henry's writing is _____ bad.

5. My uncle is _____ generous.

6. Mr. Thompson is _____ old. (He is 87 years old.)

7. This suit is _____ old; I can't wear it any more.

8. The traffic officer arrested Tom because he was driving _____ fast.

9. Don was _____ sick. They had to take him to the hospital.

10. He was _____ sick to go in a taxi. They had to call an ambulance.

11. Johnny ate _____ much and became ill.

12. Helen loves her parents _____ much.

Dialog

Do you enjoy watching television?

Yes, but I don't like some of the programs.

There are some programs that I don't like, either. Some of them are pretty silly.

Sometimes there are very good shows at eleven p.m., but that's too late for me.

LESSON XX

Ask (interrogate, inquire), **ask for** *(request), and* **ask** *plus Noun or Pronoun with Infinitive—***like** *and* **alike***—"I am glad" and "I am sorry" Followed by Infinitive or Clause*

The verb **ask** has several different meanings, which we will study and practice in this lesson. First, look up the definitions of these words:

another _____   help (*verb* and *noun*) _____

bill _____   lend _____

date (appointment) _____   price _____

explain _____   waiter (*feminine:* waitress) _____

Ask means to *interrogate* or to *inquire.*

It may be used with a direct object:

He *asked* my name.
He *asked* a question.

It may also be used with an indirect object:

He *asked me* a question.

It is often followed by the preposition *about:*

They *asked about* the meeting.

Exercise A.   Answer the following questions. Remember that "asked" is a one-syllable word.

1. Does James ask
   many questions?

Yes, he asks _____.

No, he does not ask

_____.

2. Did you ask
   about the bus?
          it

Yes, I asked _____.

No, I _____.

3. Will you ask
   Helen where she
   her
   lives?

Yes, _____.

No, I _____.

4. Are you going to
   ask another
   question?

Yes, _____.

No, I _____.

5. Did you ask the
   price of the
   shoes?

Yes, _____.

No, I _____.

Exercise B.   **Ask for** means to *request:*

1. Does Tom ask for help with his lessons?

     Yes, _____.

2. Does he ask you for help?

     Yes, he asks me _____.

3. Does Alice ask her father for money?
                   him

     Yes, _____.

4. Did you ask the waiter for the bill?
             him

     Yes, I asked _____.

5. Did Tom ask Alice for a date?
             her

100

Yes, _____.

6. Is he going to ask her for a date?

Yes, _____.

Answer "No" to the same questions:

No, he doesn't ask for _____.

No, he _____.

No, she _____.

No, I _____.

No, he _____.

No, he _____.

Exercise C. **Ask** plus a noun or pronoun with infinitive means *to request someone to do something:*

1. Does Tom ask you to help him?
    Yes, he asks me to help him.
2. Did he ask you to explain the lesson?

    Yes, _____.
3. Did he ask you to lend him ten dollars ($10)?

    Yes, _____.
4. Did you ask Tom to go with you?
               him
    Yes, I asked him to go with me.
5. Did he ask Helen to go with him?
             her

    Yes, _____.
6. Are you going to ask Mr. and Mrs. Brown to pay for the tickets?
                  them

    Yes, _____.

Answer "No" to the same questions:

No, he doesn't ask me _____ .

No, he didn't _____ .

No, _____ .

No, _____ .

No, _____ .

No, _____ .

The following words will be in the next exercise:

camera	_____	watch (noun)	_____
cowboy	_____	wine	_____
exact (adjective)	_____	look (have an appearance)	_____
pen	_____	sound (make a noise)	_____
vinegar	_____	taste (have a flavor)	_____

Like and *Alike*

Distinguish carefully between **alike** and **like**. **Like** means "similar to," and it is a preposition in its function. Used in this way, it takes an object:

Your watch is *like mine.*	(Your watch is *similar to mine.*)
John looks *like his father.*	(John has an appearance *similar to his father's.*)
That sounds *like a jet plane.*	(That makes a noise similar to the noise of a *jet plane.*)
Your car is *just like ours.*	(Your car is *exactly similar to ours.*)

Alike is an adjective or an adverb, and it *always refers back to a plural subject or plural form of the verb.* It means "similar" or "in a similar manner."

Your watch and mine *are alike*. (The two watches are similar.)

John and his father *look alike*. (They have a similar appearance.)

Exercise D. Write the correct word (**like** or **alike**) in the blank spaces:

1. Henry's pen is _____ Jim's.

2. Their pens are _____ .

3. Frank dresses _____ a cowboy.

4. This wine tastes _____ vinegar.

5. Helen and her sister dress _____ .

6. Our new car is just _____ yours.

7. The two cars are exactly _____ .

8. That sounds _____ my telephone.

9. The two brothers look _____ .

10. That looks _____ John's handwriting.

Complete the second sentence in each pair, *adding any essential words:*

11. Jim looks like his brother.

    The two brothers _____ _____ .
12. Your camera and Philip's are alike.

    Your camera is _____ _____ .
13. Jane dresses like her sister.

    Jane and her sister _____ _____ .
14. My uncle's apartment and ours are alike.

    My uncle's apartment is _____ _____ .

"*I am glad*" and "*I am sorry*" Followed by Infinitive or Clause

I am glad _____ I am sorry _____

These expressions may be followed *by an infinitive* or *by a clause:*

     FOLLOWED BY CLAUSE

I am glad to see you.   I am glad that I came.
I am glad to know that you are well.   I am glad that you are here.

I am sorry to leave early.   I am sorry that I didn't see you.
I am sorry to hear that John is sick.   I am sorry that you can't stay.

Exercise E.   Complete the following sentences, *using the infinitive:*

1. I am glad to _____ .

2. I am glad to _____ .

3. I am sorry to _____ .

4. I am sorry to _____ .

Complete the following sentences, *using a clause:*

5. I am glad that _____ .

6. I am glad that _____ .

7. I am sorry that _____ .

8. I am sorry that _____ .

Dialog

Did you ask the manager for a vacation this summer?
Yes, and I'm glad that I can take it very soon. I plan to leave next week.
I hope you can take a lot of good pictures this year.
I hope so, too. I have a fine camera, just like yours.

LESSON XXI

Structure Drills on **have to, plan to, hope to, want to**—**want** *plus Noun or Pronoun with Infinitive—Measurements of Time and Space with Corresponding Adjectives—***how long? how old? how wide?** *etc.*

hope (*verb*) _____   plan (*verb*) _____

The adjective **long**, *when it refers to time*, may also be an adverb. For example:

> *how long?*—for how much time? (See Lesson X, p. 45.)
> *longer*—for a longer time

Exercise A.

have to (See Lesson XI, p. 53.)
1. Does George have to be here every day?

   Yes, he has to _____.

   No, he doesn't have to _____.
2. Do you have to stay here much longer?

   Yes, _____.

   No, _____.
3. Did Frank have to work last night?

   Yes, _____.

   No, _____.

4. Will they have to pay the bill tomorrow?

    Yes, _____.

    No, _____.

plan to

5. Do you plan to go with John?

    Yes, _____.

    No, _____.

6. Does he plan to drive his car?

    Yes, _____.

    No, _____.

7. Do you and John plan to come back tomorrow?

    Yes, we _____.

    No, _____.

8. Do your friends plan to leave next week?

    Yes, they _____.

    No, _____.

hope to

9. Do you hope to take your vacation soon?

    Yes, _____.

    No, _____.

10. Does Richard hope to find a new job?

    Yes, _____.

    No, _____.

11. Do Mr. and Mrs. Davis hope to sell their house?

    Yes, they _____.

    No, _____.

want to   (See Lesson XIX, p. 94.)

12. Do you want to stay downtown?

Yes, _____.

No, _____.

13. Does Helen want to go to the dance?

Yes, _____.

No, _____.

14. Do the children want to go to bed now?

Yes, they _____.

No, _____.

Want plus Noun or Pronoun with Infinitive

Refer to Lesson XX, p. 101:

> Tom *asks* me to help him.
> Compare: Tom *wants* me to help him.

Exercise B.

1. Does Grace want you to help her?   Yes, she wants me to help her.

   No, she doesn't want me to help her.

2. Does your father want you to drive the car?   Yes, he _____.

   No, he _____.

3. Do you want Tom to drive?   Yes, _____.
           him

   No, _____.

4. Does Henry want you to buy his car?   Yes, _____.

   No, _____.

5. Does your uncle want you to visit him?   Yes, he _____.

   No, _____.

6. Do you want your friends to go with you?　　　Yes, I want them to
　　　　　 ⏜
　　　　　them
　　　　　　　　　　　　　　　　　　　　　　　　　go with me.

　　No, I _____.

Measurements of Time and Space with Corresponding Adjectives

The following pairs are composed of *opposite* adjectives. Write their meaning:

{ old　　_____　　　　　　　{ tall　_____

　young _____　　　　　　　　 short _____

{ wide　_____　　　　　　　{ long　_____

　narrow _____　　　　　　　　 short _____

{ old　　_____　　　　　　　{ high　_____

　new　 _____　　　　　　　　 low　 _____

{ deep　_____　　　　　　　{ thick _____

　shallow _____　　　　　　　 thin　_____

The following are measurements of time and space with plural forms. Write their meaning:

| year _____ | month _____ | inch _____ | foot _____ |
| years | months | inches | feet |

| yard _____ | mile _____ | story (This word refers to the |
| yards | miles | height of a building, and |

story (This word refers to the height of a building, and indicates *one floor*. The plural form is *stories*.) (British spelling is *storey, storeys*.)

Exercise C.　Answer the following questions, using the words given above:

1. How *old* is Helen?　　　　　She is seventeen years *old*.

2. How *long* is the table?　　　It is _____ *long*.

3. How *tall* is Frank?　　　　　He is _____ *tall*.

4. How *wide* is the cloth?   It is _____ _____ .

5. How *deep* is the lake?   _____ .

6. How *high* is the building?   _____ . (stories)

7. How *thick* is the wall?   _____ .

8. How *old* is Mr. Taylor?   _____ .

9. How *tall* is he?   _____ .

10. How *long* is the boat?   _____ .

11. How *wide* is the street?   _____ .

12. How *deep* is the river?   _____ .

13. How *thick* is the book?   _____ .

14. How *high* is the mountain?   _____ .

15. How *high* is the hotel?   _____ .

Dialog

How high is the new building going to be?

They say it's going to be thirty stories high. Mr. Smith plans to open an office there.

Did he ask you to work for him?

Yes, he asked me to work for him, but I don't have to give him an answer now.

LESSON XXII

Past Tense, Regular and Irregular—Continuous Form of Past Tense—Talking about the Weather

Review past tense forms at the beginning of Lesson IX, page 37. Also review Forms 1, 2, and 3 of the past tense of the verbs **be** and **work**, Appendix 1, pages 250 and 254.

Regular verbs form the past tense by adding "ed":

work, work**ed**   enjoy, enjoy**ed**   travel, travel**ed**

If a verb ends in "e," only a "d" is added:

live, live**d**   like, like**d**   change, change**d**

If the verb ends in "y" *after a consonant*, change "y" to "i" and add "ed":

study, stud**ied**   marry, marr**ied**   cry, cr**ied**

Exercise A. Write the past tense forms of the following *regular* verbs, according to the above rules of spelling:

PRESENT	PAST	PRESENT	PAST
answer		cook	
arrive		dance	
belong		dress	
call		enjoy	

PRESENT	PAST	PRESENT	PAST
learn	_____	shout	_____
like	_____	stay	_____
listen	_____	study	_____
live	_____	talk	_____
look	_____	travel	_____
move	_____	use	_____
rain	_____	visit*	_____
reach	_____	wait*	_____
receive	_____	want*	_____
rent*	_____	watch	_____
sew	_____	work	_____

Write the past tense forms of the following *irregular* verbs. (See pages 260–261, Appendix 1.)

PRESENT	PAST	PRESENT	PAST
be	_____	eat	_____
bring	_____	find	_____
buy	_____	fly	_____
can	_____	get	_____
come	_____	give	_____
cost	_____	go	_____
do	_____	have	_____
drive	_____	hear	_____

*The "ed" forms a separate syllable *only when the original verb ends in "t" or "d."*

PRESENT	PAST	PRESENT	PAST
know	_____	sell	_____
leave	_____	send	_____
lend	_____	sing	_____
make	_____	sit	_____
pay	_____	speak	_____
put	_____	take	_____
run	_____	wear	_____
see	_____	write	_____

Exercise B. Change the following sentences from affirmative to negative:

FORM 1

FORM 3

1. Henry went with us.

Henry did not go with us.

2. It rained last night.

_____.

3. She spoke to me.

_____.

4. The hat cost seven dollars.

_____.

5. We drove fast.

_____.

6. I found my pen.

_____.

7. He wore his raincoat.

_____.

8. He studied very hard.

_____.

Change the following sentences from negative to affirmative:

FORM 3

FORM 1

9. He did not pay the bill.

He paid the bill.

10. They did not arrive on time.

_____.

11. I did not send the letter.

_____.

112

	Form 3	Form 1

12.	I was not there.	_____ .
13.	We could not see it.*	_____ .
14.	We did not leave early.	_____ .
15.	She did not rent the house.	_____ .
16.	He did not get up early.	_____ .

Continuous Form of Past Tense

Study the past tense, Forms 5, 6, and 7 (Appendix 1, pp. 250 and 254–255).

Form 5	Form 6	Form 7
I was studying	was I studying?	I was not studying
you were studying	were you studying?	you were not studying
he was studying	was he studying?	he was not studying
we were studying	were we studying?	we were not studying
you were studying	were you studying?	you were not studying
they were studying	were they studying?	they were not studying

These forms describe an action which *was continuing in the past*, when another action occurred or was taking place.

Henry was taking a bath
when the telephone rang.

Alice was feeding the dog
when John opened the door.

What *were you doing* when John
opened the door?   _____ .

What *were you doing* when the
telephone rang?   _____ .

*Remember that **can**, like **be**, *does not* use the auxiliaries *do, does,* or *did* in the *negative* forms.

113

Exercise C. Answer the following questions, using Forms 5 and 7, as indicated.

1. Were you studying when the doorbell rang? Yes, _____.

   No, _____.

2. Was Henry taking a nap when his friends arrived? Yes, _____.

   No, _____.

3. Was it raining when Mr. Palmer left the office? Yes, _____.

   No, _____.

4. Was Tom driving when the accident happened? Yes, _____.

   No, _____.

5. What were you doing when Jenny saw you? I was _____.

6. What was Tom doing when the telephone rang? He _____.

7. What was Mrs. Brown doing when the children came home from school? She _____.

Talking about the Weather

rain (*noun*)	_____	cool	_____
rain (*verb*)*	_____	warm	_____
rainy	_____		
cloud	_____	cold	_____
cloudy	_____	hot	_____
wind (*noun*)	_____		

Rain is a regular verb, and the past tense is *rained* (one syllable).

114

windy _____ dry _____

shine* _____ wet _____

The impersonal pronoun **it** is used to refer to the weather:

> *It* is warm today. *It* is not raining now.
> *It* was cool yesterday. *It* rained last night.

Exercise D. Answer these questions according to actual weather conditions:

1. Is it warm today? _____.

2. Was it warm yesterday? _____.

3. Was it cool last night? _____.

4. Was it cold last January? _____.

5. Is it raining now? _____.

6. Did it rain last Sunday? _____.

7. Is the sun shining now? _____.

8. Did the sun shine yesterday? _____.

9. Was it windy last night? _____.

10. Was it rainy last weekend? _____.

11. Was it cloudy when you got up this morning? _____.

12. Was the sun shining when you got up? _____.

13. Was it raining when you left the house? _____.

*When we use the verb *shine*, the subject is *the sun*. For example:

> The sun is shining now. The sun shone (past irregular) yesterday.

115

Dialog

What were you doing last night when I called you up?

When you called me up, I was reading. I didn't want to go out because it was raining.

I was studying when it started to rain. Then I decided to stay at home.

It may rain again tonight. The weather report says "Cloudy and cool with possible thunder showers."

LESSON XXIII

*Present and Past Tenses, Simple and Continuous Forms—Negative Questions—Direct and Indirect Objects of the Verb—**other, another, the other—else***

introduce	_____	game	_____
fall*	_____	glasses (eyeglasses)	_____
lose*	_____	husband	_____
read*	_____	wife	_____
say*	_____	manager	_____
tell*	_____	truth	_____

Exercise A.   Review the present and past tenses, simple and continuous forms:

1. Does George wear glasses?   Yes, _____ .

2. Is he wearing his glasses now?   No, _____ .

3. Did he wear glasses last year?   Yes, _____ .
4. Was he wearing his glasses
   when he fell down?   Yes, _____ .

*See pages 260–261, Appendix 1, for irregular past tense.

5. Does Jenny write many
   letters?   No, _____ .

6. Is she writing a letter now?   Yes, _____ .
7. Did she write you a letter last
   week?   Yes, _____ .
8. Was she writing letters when
   the phone rang?   No, _____ .

Negative Questions

Study the *negative questions*, Forms 4 and 8, present and past
tenses, on pages 249, 250, 254, and 255, Appendix 1. These negative
questions *almost always* (with the exception of the first person singular) *use the verbal contractions:*

FORM 2	FORM 4
Does George wear glasses?	Doesn't George wear glasses?

FORM 6	FORM 8
Were they eating dinner?	Weren't they eating dinner?

Exercise B.   Change the following *affirmative* questions *to negative:*

FORM 2 OR 6   FORM 4 OR 8
1. Does Grace take lessons?   Doesn't Grace _____ ?

2. Is the child taking a nap now? _____ ?

3. Did you lose your pen?   _____ ?

4. Were you reading the paper?   _____ ?

Change to *negative*, and begin the question with "Why."

5. Does Miss Parker wear
   glasses?   Why doesn't Miss Parker _____ ?
6. Are they bringing their
   children?   Why _____ ?

7. Did he send the letter?   Why _____ ?

8. Was Jim studying his lesson?   Why _____ ?

118

Direct and Indirect Objects of the Verb

Henry ——→ gave ——→ the flowers ——→ to Olga.

subject   verb   direct object   indirect object

If the *direct object* is a *pronoun*, like "it" or "them," it *must follow the verb, and cannot be separated from it:*

Henry ————→ gave ————→ them ————→ to Olga.

Exercise C.   Change the italicized direct object to a pronoun:

1. John gave *the book* to me.   John gave *it* to me.
2. George sent *the letter* to his father.   _____.
3. Mr. Jones bought *the gloves* for his wife.   _____.
4. Jenny lent *her book* to George.   _____.
5. Mr. and Mrs. Allen sold *their car* to us.   _____.
6. Dick introduced *Herbert* to the teacher.   _____.
7. Henry took *my brother and me* to the game.   _____.
8. He bought *the tickets* for us.   _____.
9. I bought *the flowers* for you.   _____.

If the *direct object* is a *noun*, there are *two* possible word orders.

Henry ——→ gave ——→ the flowers ——→ to Olga.

subject   verb   direct object   indirect object

Henry ——→ gave ——→ Olga ——→ the flowers.

subject   verb   indirect object   direct object

In such constructions, for the second form to be possible, the *direct object* must be a *noun*, but the *indirect object* may be either a *noun* or a *pronoun:*

Henry gave the flowers to her.
Henry gave her the flowers.

Exercise D. Change the word order of each of the following sentences. Do not change the *words*—change only the *order* of the words. Use the preposition **to** before the indirect object *when it is separated from the verb.*

1. Helen gave me the books.   Helen gave the books *to me*.

2. Albert lent my brother $25.   _____.
3. Frank sold George his tickets.   _____.

4. Mr. Adams sold us his car.   _____.
5. Mr. Thomas wrote his wife a letter.   _____.

6. He told her the truth.   _____.
7. We brought him the package.   _____.

8. Frank sold his house to Mr. Finch.   Frank sold Mr. Finch his house.

9. Alice gave the tickets to me.   _____.
10. George sent a telegram to his father.   _____.
11. She bought a book for her husband.   _____.
12. Henry told the truth to his cousin.   _____.
13. Albert lent ten dollars to his friend.   _____.
14. He wrote a letter to the manager.   _____.

Other, Another, The Other

cheap _____   key _____   tea _____

expensive _____   son _____   third (3d) _____

drink _____   prefer _____

120

Other (meaning *additional* or *different*) is an *adjective* as well as a *pronoun*.

	SINGULAR	PLURAL
As an *adjective*, it may be used		
with an *indefinite* article	———— another* book	other books
with a *definite* article	———— the other book	the other books

As a *pronoun*, it may be used

with an *indefinite* article	———— another*	others
with a *definite* article	———— the other	the others

In the *plural* (*indefinite*) **other** is frequently preceded by **some**:

some other books   some others

As an *adjective*, **other** is frequently followed by the pronoun **one** or **ones**:

another one, the other one, other ones, the other ones, some other ones

Exercise E. Fill in the blanks as indicated in parentheses. Distinguish carefully between *singular* and *plural:*

1. Would you like _____ cup of coffee?
   (*adjective indefinite*)

2. This pen costs five dollars. Don't they have

   _____ pens that are cheaper?
   (*adjective indefinite*)

3. I like _____ apartment better than this one.
   (*adjective definite*)

4. He has three sons; one is a doctor, and

   _____ two sons are teachers.
   (*adjective definite*)

*Note that "an other" is written as one word: *another*.

121

5. He has three sons; one is a doctor, _____

                                            (*pronoun indefinite*)

is a teacher, and the third is still in school.

6. Some people drink coffee. _____ prefer tea.

                             (*pronoun indefinite*)

7. We have two keys. I have one. Do you have _____?

                                           (*pronoun definite*)

8. Only a few students are here. Where are _____?

                                          (*pronoun definite*)

Else

One may also use the adjective **else** to mean "other." For example, "someone else" means "some other person"; "anything else" means "any other thing." **Else** may be used in this way after the following words:

someone else	everyone else	something else
somebody else	everybody else	anything else
anyone else	no one else	nothing else
anybody else	nobody else	everything else

Exercise F. From the *above list*, fill in the blanks in the following sentences:

1. John wants to talk with Mr. Brown. He will not talk with _____.

2. Mr. Brown was out of town, so John had to talk with _____.

3. They didn't have any apple pie, so I ate _____.

4. Frank didn't come to the party, but _____
(all the others) came.

5. I don't like Coca-Cola. Don't you have _____?

Else may also be used in these interrogative expressions:

who else? what else? when else? where else?
why else? how else?

John has a key to the office. *Who else* has a key?
Betty can type, but *what else* can she do?

They traveled in Greece. *Where else* did they go?
We don't want to take a plane. *How else* can we get to
Trinidad?

He can't come on Friday. _____ _____ can he come?

Helen is probably sick. _____ _____ would she be absent
from the class?

_____ _____ do you have to do before you leave the
office?

As an *adverb*, **else** is used in: *somewhere else* (in or to another
place), *anywhere else* (in or to any other place), and *nowhere else* (in
or to no other place).

It is too warm here. We want to go _____ _____ .
We stayed in London all the time. We didn't go

_____ _____ .

He wants to stay in Paris. He is happy _____ _____ .

Dialog

Don't you think I look like my grandfather?
No, you look more like your mother.
It was my mother's birthday yesterday. I gave her a big box of
candy.
What are you going to give me on my birthday?
I haven't decided. Maybe I'll just give you some good advice.

LESSON XXIV

*Drill on Continuous Form of Past Tense—Past Tense of **going to**—say and.tell—**usually** and **used to***

Present	Past
call up (to telephone) _____	called up
get home (to arrive at home) _____	got home
forget _____	forgot
sleep _____	slept
start _____	started (two syllables)
change _____	changed (one syllable)

to change one's mind (to change one's opinion or intention) _____

out of order (not functioning, not in good order) _____

enough (sufficient) _____   instead (as an alternative) _____

Exercise A.   Review the continuous forms of the past tense (Forms 5, 6, and 7).

1. Was Henry studying when you called him up?

Yes, he _____.

No, he _____.

2. Were you sleeping when it started to rain?

      Yes, I _____ .

      No, I _____ .

3. Was it raining when you looked out (of) the window?

      Yes, it _____ .

      No, it _____ .

4. What were you doing at half-past six last night?

      I was _____ .

5. What was your brother doing when you got home?

      He _____ .

6. What was Helen doing when you called her up?

      She _____ .

Past Tense of *Going to*

In Lesson XVII, page 83, we used the *present continuous* form of **go** to express *future time:*

> Henry *is going to buy* a car next month.
> I *am going to pay* for the tickets tomorrow.

The *past continuous* form of **go** may be used to indicate that one *intended* to do something in the *past*, but did *not* do it:

> I *was going to study*, but I didn't.
> You *were going to write* the letter, but you didn't.
> They *were going to sell* their house, but they didn't.

Used in this way, "was going to" means "intended to."

Exercise B. Rewrite the following sentences, changing "intended" to "was going" or "were going":

1. I intended to study, but I went to the movies instead.

      I was going to study, but _____ .

2. I intended to eat lunch downtown, but I changed my mind.

      I _____

3. He intended to buy the car, but he didn't have enough money.

   _____.

4. She intended to wear her new hat, but it rained.

   _____.

5. I intended to write the letter, but I forgot it.

   _____.

6. We intended to go to bed early, but some visitors arrived.

   _____.

7. They intended to watch television, but the TV set was out of order.

   _____.

The Verbs *Say* and *Tell*

	PRESENT	PAST
say	_____	said
tell	_____	told

Always use **say** with a direct quotation*:

> The baby can say "Daddy" and "Mama."
> John said to me, "I have a new job."

Always use **say** with an indirect quotation (one without quotation marks) *when there is not any indirect object:*

> John said that he had a new job.
> John said he had a new job. (The conjunction **that** may be omitted.)

If there is an *indirect object before the indirect quotation*, you *must use* **tell**:

> John told *Henry* (that) he had a new job.
> John told *me* that he had a new job.

Use **tell** to express a command if the indirect object is followed by an infinitive:

> John told Henry to call him up.
> John told me to write the letter.

*A direct quotation is one with which quotation marks ("...") are used.

126

Exercise C. Answer the following questions:

1. Did Henry say "Good morning" to Florence?

Yes, he said _____.   No, he didn't say __.

2. Did your brother say (that) he could come?

Yes, _____.   No, _____.

3. Did Frank tell you (that) he had a cold?

Yes, _____.   No, _____.

4. Did Mr. and Mrs. Wells tell you about their trip?

Yes, _____.   No, _____.

5. Did you tell Frank to come to the meeting?

Yes, _____.   No, _____.

Exercise D. The following sentences are all in the *past* tense. Fill in the blanks with the correct form of **say** or **tell**:

1. Barbara _____, "I can go with you."

2. Barbara _____ she could go with us.

3. Barbara _____ me that she could go with us.

4. Did Frank _____ you (that) he had a new car?

5. What did Mr. Smith _____?

6. What did Mr. Smith _____ his friend?

7. Betty didn't _____ her mother where she went.

8. She _____ us that she bought a new dress yesterday.

9. She _____ that it was not expensive.

10. What did John _____ when you _____ him that

you had his book?

Usually and Used to

If you refer to a *customary action in the present*, say **usually***:

> I usually get up early.
> Jim doesn't usually wear a hat.
> Do you usually take a taxi?

The phrase **used to,** preceded by a subject and followed by a verb, e.g.,

> "John used to play tennis"

signifies something which the subject does not do now, but which he did customarily in the past. "John used to play tennis" means that John *does not play tennis now*, but that *it was his custom to play tennis in the past.*

> Mr. Smith doesn't smoke now, but he *used to smoke.*
> Henry doesn't live in Miami now, but he *used to live there.*

Forms 2, 3, and 4 of "used to" are regular:

> Did he use to smoke?   He didn't use to smoke.
> Didn't he use to smoke?

Exercise E.   Fill in the blanks with **usually** or **used to**.   Remember that **used to** *cannot* be used in the *present* tense—it always indicates past time.

1. Dick smokes cigarettes now, but he _____ smoke a pipe.

2. He _____ buys his cigarettes at the drugstore.

3. Helen is slender now, but she _____ be fat.

4. John works at the bank now, and he _____ takes the 8:30

bus, so I never see him. He _____ work at the post

*Usually, like other adverbs, may be used with a verb in any tense.

office, and I _____ see him every morning on the 9 o'clock bus.

5. The child _____ takes a nap after lunch. I _____ take a nap every day, but now I don't have time.

6. Henry lives with his uncle now, but he _____ have a small apartment. When he lived in the apartment, he _____ cooked his own meals.

7. Miss Harris _____ wear bright colors, but now, since her father died, she _____ wears white or black.

Dialog

Does Henry usually tell you about his vacation plans?

He always used to tell me, but this year he has said nothing about his vacation.

I heard him say he was going to Florida.

I used to go to Florida, but now I prefer to go to the mountains. I usually go in August.

Well, don't tell Henry that I said anything about it.

LESSON XXV

Present Perfect Tense, Simple and Continuous Forms—Verbal Contractions in the Present Perfect Tense—no Substituted for not any

ago _____   bicycle _____   guest _____

bath _____   drawer_____   sky _____

go to sleep (begin to sleep, fall asleep) _____

The three parts of the verb must be learned now. If the verb is *regular*, the third part (which we call the *past participle*) is the same as the simple past:

   rain, *rained*, **rained**   live, *lived*, **lived**
   work, *worked*, **worked**   study, *studied*, **studied**

If the verb is *irregular*, the third part is *sometimes* different from the second. Many irregular verbs are listed on pp. 260–261, Appendix 1. Find the *third part* (the *past participle*) of the following verbs, and write it in the blank space:

   be   *was*   _____

   go   *went*   _____

   have   *had*   _____

   sell   *sold*   _____

| sleep | *slept* | _____ |
| take | *took* | _____ |

Exercise A. Look at the present perfect tense on pp. 251 and 255–256, Appendix 1, and study Forms 1, 2, and 3. Then answer the following questions:

1. Have you been in Canada?*

Yes, _____.   No,_____.

2. Has Albert studied his lesson?

Yes, _____.   No, _____.

3. Has Johnny taken his bath?

Yes, _____.   No, _____.

4. Have Mr. and Mrs. Roberts sold their house?

Yes, _____.   No, _____.

In the preceding sentences, the present perfect tense expresses *indefinite* time in the *past*. Used in this way, it is not very different from the *simple past*. For example, the following sentences are practically the same in meaning:

They have sold their house.   (*present perfect*)
They sold their house.   (*past*)

However, if *a specific time in the past* is mentioned, the *past tense must be used:*

They sold their house *last week.*

Exercise B. Fill in the proper form of the verb indicated:

PRESENT PERFECT   PAST

1. We _____ in Washington.   1a. We _____ in Washington
   (*be*)   (*be*)
                                    in 1968.

*The past participle *been* is often followed by the preposition "to" in place of "in," e.g., "Have you been to Canada?" The use of **to** instead of **in** is restricted to verb forms that end with **been**.

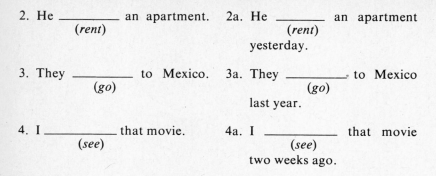

2. He _____ an apartment.   2a. He _____ an apartment
      (rent)   (rent)
                           yesterday.

3. They _____ to Mexico.   3a. They _____ to Mexico
      (go)   (go)
                           last year.

4. I _____ that movie.   4a. I _____ that movie
    (see)   (see)
                           two weeks ago.

In the following situations, the present perfect tense *must be used* to describe an action which *began in the past and continues into the present.* In this situation, *no other tense is acceptable in English.**

      Mr. and Mrs. Brown *have* a house which they *bought* ten
                (present)   (past)
years ago.
      Mr. and Mrs. Brown *have had* their house *for ten years.*
      (present perfect)

Miss Anderson *lives* in Miami. She *went* there to live six months ago.
      Miss Anderson *has lived* in Miami for *six months.*

Albert *works* at the bank. He *started* to work there in 1965.
Albert *has worked* at the bank *since 1965.*

Bob and Betty *are* married. They *got* married last June.
Bob and Betty *have been* married *since last June.*

Exercise C. Complete the following sentences, using the present perfect tense:

1. Mr. and Mrs. Cooper are at the Hilton Hotel. They came three days ago.

    They _____ for three days.

*In several other languages, the present tense is used in this situation. Be very careful to avoid this usage in English.

132

2. My little brother has a bicycle. We gave it to him two months ago.

My little brother _____ for two months.

3. We have guests at our house. They came yesterday.

We _____ since yesterday.

4. Nancy takes music lessons. She began her lessons last April.

Nancy _____ since last April.

In the present perfect tense, there is very little difference in meaning between the *simple* forms (Forms 1, 2, and 3) and the *continuous* (Forms 5, 6, and 7). In the following sentences, use Form 5 instead of Form 1:

5. Henry is working at the post office. He started to work there two weeks ago.

Henry _____ for two weeks.

6. The baby is sleeping. He went to sleep half an hour ago.

The baby _____ for half an hour.

7. The baby is sleeping. He went to sleep at half-past two.

The baby _____ since half-past two.

8. It is raining. It started to rain last night.

It _____ since last night.

Verbal Contractions in the **Present Perfect Tense:**

I have been	I've been	I have not been	I haven't been
you have gone	you've gone	you have not gone	you haven't gone
he has had, she had had, it has had	he's had, she's* had, it's had	he has not had, she has not had, etc.	he hasn't had, she hasn't had, it hasn't had
we have seen	we've seen	we have not seen	we haven't seen
they have sold	they've sold	they have not sold	they haven't sold

No Substituted for *Not Any*

The negative form "not any" has already been used. (Lesson V, page 20). It is possible to use the adjective "no" in place of "not

*Note that "he's, she's, it's" are contractions of the pronoun plus "has" *or* "is":

He is here now. = He's here now.   He has been here. = He's been here.
It is raining. = It's raining.   It has rained all day. = It's rained all day.

133

any." If "no" is used, the preceding verb must be in *affirmative*, not negative, form, because "no" makes the sentence negative in meaning, and in English *we cannot use two negatives in the same clause.*

There is *not any* milk in the refrigerator.
There is *no* milk in the refrigerator.

There are *not any* children in the class.
There are *no* children in the class.

Helen does *not* have *any* notebook.
Helen has *no* notebook.

I did *not* buy *any* flowers.
I bought *no* flowers.

Exercise D.   Rewrite each sentence, using "no" in place of "not any":

1. There isn't any telephone in the office.

    _____.

2. There weren't any people in the room.

    _____.

3. I didn't find any money in the drawer.

    _____.

4. They didn't see any interesting shows in New York.

    _____.

5. Mrs. Baker doesn't have any friends in Chicago.

    _____.

6. Henry doesn't ask any questions.

    _____.

7. I don't see any clouds in the sky.

    _____.

Dialog

Are John and Betty married?
Yes, they've been married for two months.

Where are they living?

They're living at the hotel because they haven't bought their furniture yet.

Have you seen John lately?

No, I haven't seen him since he got married.

LESSON XXVI

*Use of Present Perfect Tense—**already,** **still, yet**—Structure Drill on First Four Tenses*

In Lesson XXV, you used the *present perfect tense* with phrases like:

for three months   since last April

This is the natural and customary use of the present perfect tense in English. This tense *must not be used* with the word **ago.** **Ago** points toward a definite time in the past, and is used *only with a past tense:*

I bought my car *two years ago.*

Use the present perfect tense to say:

I have had my car *for two years.*
I have had my car *since 19—.*

PRESENT TENSE	PAST TENSE	PAST PARTICIPLE
be	was	been
know	knew	known
see	saw	seen
wear	wore	worn

Exercise A.   In the following sentences, note the relationship between the present tense and the present perfect:

1. Do Mr. and Mrs. Brown live in Chicago now?   Yes, they *live*

———————————— .

1a. How long have they lived in Chicago? They *have lived*

_____.

2. Do you know Henry Gibbs? Yes, _____.

    2a. How long have you known him? _____.

3. Is your cousin sick? Yes, _____.

    3a. How long has he been sick? _____.

4. Is Dick waiting for Barbara? Yes, _____.

    4a. How long has he been waiting for her?_____.

5. Does Mr. Parker wear glasses? Yes, _____.

    5a. How long has he worn glasses? _____.

6. Does Bob's father have a grocery store?   Yes, _____.

    6a. How long has he had his store? _____.

Already, Yet, and Still

Already, yet, and **still** are adverbs that are similar, but not identical, in meaning. The differences in the use of these three adverbs can only be learned through practice, but these explanations will help you:

Already means "previously." It is used most frequently with the present perfect tense, in sentences like those in Exercise A, page 131. It is *not* to be used, however, with the negative verb.

Yet means "up to the present time." Like **already,** it is used most frequently with the present perfect tense. However, **yet** is almost never used with an affirmative verb.

Both **already** and **yet** may be used in the interrogative form, but note the possible differences in word order:

        Has Albert **already** studied his lesson?
        Has Albert studied his lesson **yet**?
Yes, he has **already** studied his lesson.

           No, he has **not yet** studied his lesson.
           No, he has **not** studied his lesson **yet**.

Has Helen learned to drive **yet**?
Yes, she has **already** learned to drive.

No, she has **not** learned to drive **yet**.

Already and **yet** refer to time that *ends with the present.* **Still** begins in the past, but *continues into the present time*, and is therefore most frequently used with the *present tense.* In the *negative*, **still** is sometimes, but not always, replaced by **now, any more,** or **any longer.**

Do they **still** live in Miami?
Yes, they **still** live in Miami.   No, they don't live in Miami **now**.
Is Dick **still** waiting for Barbara?
Yes, he is **still** waiting for her. No, he isn't waiting for her **any longer.**

PAST   PRESENT   FUTURE
          already
— — — → — — — → — — — → — →
       (not) yet
— — — → — — — → — — — → — — →
              still
— — — — → — — → — — → — — → → — — → —

Exercise B.   Fill in the blanks with **already, still,** or **yet:**

1. Have you _____ written the letter?

2. Have you written the letter _____?

3. Henry has not _____ taken the examination.

4. Does he _____ study English at the university?

5. They have _____ left for Europe.

6. They have not sold their house _____.

7. My uncle is _____ in Washington.

8. He has not _____ bought a car.

9. He is _____ planning to buy a used car.

10. His father has _____ given him the money.

Structure Drill on First Four Tenses

In Lesson XXI, pp. 105–107, you used the verbs **have, want, plan,** and **hope** followed by an infinitive. The verbs **try** and **know how** are also followed by the infinitive.

Exercise C. **Study** and **try** are regular verbs, with the same spelling changes:

study   studied   studied   try   tried   tried

1. Do you have to study hard? Yes, _____.

   No, _____.

2. Did you have to get up early yesterday? Yes, _____.

   No, _____.

3. Will you have to get home early tonight? Yes, _____.

   No, _____.

4. Have you had to work hard since last year? Yes, _____.

   No, _____.

5. Does Henry try to answer the questions? Yes, he tries _____.

   No, he doesn't try _____.

6. Did he try to study last night? Yes, he tried _____.

   No, _____.

7. Will he try to get a job next year? Yes, _____.

   No, _____.

8. How long has Richard been trying to get a job?

   He _____ for _____.

   since _____.

139

9. Does Betty know how to drive? Yes, _____.

   No, _____.

10. Did Frank know how to drive a year ago? Yes, _____.

    No, _____.

11. How long has Mrs. Brown known how to drive?

    She _____.

12. Does Jane know how to swim? Yes, _____.

    No, _____.

13. Did Ralph know how to swim last year? Yes, _____.

    No, _____.

14. How long has Tom known how to swim?

    He _____.

Dialog

Olga has been looking for a job for almost six weeks.

What's the matter? Why can't she find one?

Perhaps it's because she doesn't know how to type. Most offices want a typist.

Couldn't she go to night school and learn to type?

Yes, she could. I'm going to suggest it to her.

LESSON XXVII

*Popular Idioms: **look for, get on, get off, put on, take off, turn on, turn off**—Compound Adjectives—**because, because of, on account of***

Exercise A.   Idioms formed with verb plus preposition:

1. look for _____

a. Is Henry looking for a job? Yes, _____.

   No, _____.

b. Are Mr. and Mrs. Lee looking for an apartment? Yes, _____.

   No, _____.

c. Were you looking for Helen last night? Yes, _____.

   No, _____.

d. How long has Mr. Rogers been looking for a secretary?

   He _____.

2. get on _____

a. Do you get on the bus on Fifth Avenue? Yes, _____.

   No, _____.

b. Did Frank get on the bus with you last night? Yes, _____.

   No, _____.

c. Is Henry going to get on the boat in Panama? Yes, _____.

No, _____.

3. get off _____

a. Does John get off the bus near his home? Yes, _____.

No, _____.

b. Did you get off the bus on Broadway yesterday? Yes, _____.

No, _____.

c. Are you going to get off at (on) the next corner? Yes, _____.

No, _____.

Exercise B. Idioms formed with verb plus *adverb:* Note that with such idioms, when the *direct object is a pronoun*, it *must follow the verb,* and not the adverb.

1. put on _____

a. Does John put on his glasses when he gets up? Yes, he puts them

on _____.

No, _____.

b. Did you put on your raincoat this morning? Yes, I put it on

_____.

No, _____.

c. Are you going to put it on before you leave? Yes, _____.

No, _____.

2. take off _____

a. Does Helen always take off her ring at night? Yes, she always

takes it off _____.

No, she doesn't always _____.

142

b. Did you take off your sweater when you came in? Yes, _____.

    No, _____.

c. Are you going to take off your coat? Yes, _____.

    No, _____.

3. turn on _____ (both _____)

a. Do you usually turn on both lights? Yes, I usually turn them both* on.

    No, _____.

b. Did Johnny turn on the water? Yes, _____.

    No, _____.

c. Are you going to turn on the heater? Yes, _____.

    No, _____.

4. turn off _____

a. Do you turn off all the lights at night? Yes, I turn them all† off

_____.

    No, _____.

b. Did you turn all of them off last night? Yes, I _____.

    No, _____.

c. Did Mr. Jones turn off the fan when he left the office? Yes, he

turned it off _____.

    No, _____.

*"Them both" may also be written "both of them." "Them both" is a pronoun and must follow the verb. "Both of them" is a noun phrase and may follow either verb or adverb.

†"Them all" may also be written "all of them." "Them all" (like "them both") is a pronoun and must follow the verb. "All of them" is a noun phrase and may follow either verb or adverb.

Compound Adjectives

A **compound adjective** is an adjective formed with two or more words joined by a hyphen or hyphens:

> a self-employed person　　an up-to-date report

Many compound adjectives are formed with a *noun and a descriptive number,* but in such cases, although the number is *plural,* the noun *must be in singular form:*

> a six-hour flight　　　　　a ten-foot pole
> a three-man team　　　　　a 25-story building

Exercise C. Rewrite the following phrases, changing the prepositional phrase to a *compound adjective with hyphen,* and placing it *before the noun:*

1. a race of five miles (a five-mile race)

2. a letter of four pages

   _____

3. a contract of two years

   _____

4. a week of forty hours

   _____

5. a house of eight rooms

   _____

6. a stamp that costs fifteen cents _____

7. a gun of twelve millimeters

   _____

8. a chain twenty inches long

   _____

9. a team of eleven men

   _____

10. a visit of five days

    _____

11. a hat that costs ten dollars

    _____

12. a baby that weighs nine pounds _____

When we refer to age, we use a special form:

> a child of four years　　　　a four-year-old child
> a house built 100 years ago　a 100-year-old house.

Because, Because of, On Account of

Review the negative questions which you studied in Lesson **XXIII,** page 118.

144

why? _____ because _____ because of _____
(on account of)

Because is a conjunction, and it is *followed by a clause:*

George stayed at home *because he was sick.*

Because of, or **on account of,** is a preposition in function, and is *followed by a noun or a noun phrase or substitute:*

George stayed at home *because of sickness.*
George stayed at home *on account of sickness.*

Exercise D. Answer the following negative questions with a complete sentence, using **because, because of,** or **on account of:**

1. Why isn't Henry looking for a job? He isn't looking for a job

   because _____.

   _____.

2. Why didn't Frank get on the bus with you? He _____

   _____.

3. Why aren't you going to get off the bus at the next corner? _____

   _____.

4. Why didn't you put on your raincoat this morning? _____

   _____.

5. Why doesn't Helen take off her ring at night? _____

   _____.

6. Why don't you turn on both lights? _____

   _____.

7. Why didn't Mr. Jones turn off the fan when he left the office?

   _____.

Dialog

Why didn't Jerry get on the bus with you?

He didn't get on with me because he was waiting for Helen.

Now that you are on the bus, you can take off your raincoat.
Plastic coats are so hot.

Yes, I'll take it off as soon as I find a seat.

LESSON XXVIII

*The Verbs **make** and **do**—Interrogative Pronouns as Subject and Object—Verb Form Following Interrogative Subject—**how much, how many?***

Make means to *fabricate* or *create*. Its three forms are: *make, made, made.*

Exercise A.

1. Does the tailor make women's suits? Yes, he _____.

   No, _____.

2. Is he making a suit for your brother? Yes, _____.

   No, _____.

3. Did Mrs. Green make a cake yesterday? Yes, _____.

   No, _____.

4. Will she make a pie tomorrow? Yes, _____.

   No, _____.

5. Does Grace know how to make candy? Yes, _____.

   No, _____.

6. Can she make good candy? Yes, _____.

   No, _____.

Do means to *perform* or *act*. Its three forms are: *do, did, done.*

Do is used frequently *without an object.* When it takes an object, that object is often the word **work** or another word that indicates a form of work.

When you use the verb **do**, remember that in the present and past tenses, Forms 2 and 3, **do** is both *principal* verb and *auxiliary* verb:

Do you always **do** your work in the morning?

Yes, I always **do** my work in the morning.
No, I **do** not always **do** my work in the morning.

Did Frank **do** the exercises yesterday?

Yes, he **did** the exercises yesterday.
No, he **did** not **do** the exercises yesterday.

Exercise B. Answer the following questions, using a form of "do":

1. Do you usually do your work before lunch? Yes, ——————— .

   No, ————————————————————— .

2. Are you doing lots of work now?* Yes, ——————— .

   No, ————————————————————— .

3. Did you do much work yesterday?* Yes, ——————— .

   No, ————————————————————— .

4. Will Henry do the work for you tomorrow? Yes, ——————— .

   No, ————————————————————— .

5. Does he know how to do the work? Yes, ——————— .

   No, ————————————————————— .

6. Is he going to do the work? Yes, ——————— .

   No, ————————————————————— .

*For **much, a lot of,** and **lots of,** see Lesson XI, page 50. Remember that "**much**" is not customarily used in an affirmative sentence.

7. Does George often do his work at night? Yes, _____.

   No, _____.

8. Is he doing good work this year? Yes, _____.

   No, _____.

9. Did he do good work last year? Yes, _____.

   No, _____.

The basic meanings of "make" and "do" are illustrated in the preceding exercises. Both verbs have other special meanings and are used in many idiomatic expressions which you must study later in a good English dictionary.

Interrogative Pronouns

SUBJECT PRONOUNS	OBJECT PRONOUNS	
who?	whom?*	"What" and "which" can also be
what?	what?	used as *adjectives*: what day? which
which?	which?	house? what places? which books?
		which one? which ones?

When you study *Form 2* of any verb, you will see that it *includes a subject:*

> was *he*? did *he* go? do *you* want? will *you* come? have *they* seen?

When you use an interrogative pronoun *as a subject,* you *cannot use Form 2* in the customary manner because you *cannot have two subjects.* For this reason, when an interrogative expression is the *subject of the question,* the usual subject in Form 2 must be omitted.

Who *went* to the meeting?   What *happened* at the meeting?
Who *didn't go?*   Which (of two paintings) *took* the prize?
What bus *stops* here?   Which one *didn't take* the prize?

*The objective form **whom** is no longer used by some English speakers, *except immediately following a preposition.* However, since this exception has to be made, and since "whom" is entirely correct and used by many speakers, it seems less complicated to learn it and use it always as the objective form.

On the contrary, when the interrogative expression is the *object of a verb* or of a *preposition*, the *regular interrogative form* (Form 2) is used:

Whom *did you see* at the meeting?

With whom *did you go*?

Which one (of two hats) *did you buy*?

Which bus *did you take*?

INTERROGATIVE SUBJECT

Who *said* that?
Who *found* the money?

INTERROGATIVE OBJECT

What *did he say*?
What *did he find*?

The interrogative expressions "how much?" and "how many?" can also be used either as *subject* or *object* of a question, following the above rules for pronouns:

How many (people) *came* to the meeting?
How much (money) *remains* in the box?
How many (people) *did you see*?
How much (money) *do you need*?

Exercise C. The word or words in *italics* in the following sentences *correspond to the interrogative pronoun or phrase*. Complete the questions, using *Form 1* if the interrogative expression is a *subject*, or *Form 2* if it is an *object*:

PRESENT TENSE

1. *John* has a question.

Who ____(has a question)____?

2. He wants to know *your address*.

What ____(does he want to know)____?

3. *Helen* wants to leave now.

Who _____?

4. She wants to buy *a pair of shoes*.

What _____?

5. *Bob's father* sells groceries.

Who _____?

6. Bob's father sells *groceries*.

What _____?

7. *Six people* live in that house.

How many people _____?

8. He needs *ten gallons of gas*.

How much gas _____?

150

9. *Ralph* gave her the candy.   Who _____ ?

10. Ralph gave her *the candy*.   What _____ ?

11. *Grace* turned on the light.   Who _____ ?

12. She turned on *the kitchen light*.   Which light _____ ?

13. *Mr. Anderson* got on the bus.   Who _____ ?

14. He got on *the Madison Street bus*.   Which bus _____ ?

15. *Henry* saw Alice at the movie.   Who _____ ?

16. Henry saw *Alice* at the movie.   Whom _____ ?

17. *Alice* said that.   Who _____ ?

18. She said, *"Good morning."*   What _____ ?

Dialog

What did you and George do last night?

We didn't do anything. We stayed at home.

We didn't go anywhere, either. Helen was sewing, and her sister was making candy.

Helen is always sewing. What is she making now?

She's making a dress for her cousin. She does very nice work.

LESSON XXIX

Conditional Sentences, Future Possible—
Idiomatic Use of it takes

as soon as _____   unless _____

if _____   until _____

    Notice in the following sentences, which indicate possible future action, that the conditional clause (the clause that follows "if," "unless," etc.) is in the *present tense:*

FUTURE TENSE		PRESENT TENSE
I will go to the beach tomorrow	if	the sun shines.
I will stay at home next Sunday	if	it rains.
Henry will pay for the tickets	if	he has enough money.
John will stay in school	until	he finishes the course.
Betty will buy the stamps	when	she goes to the post office.
We will go downtown	as soon as	it stops raining.
We will not go downtown	unless	it stops raining.

Exercise A.   Complete the conditional clauses in the following sentences, using *a verb in the present tense*:

1. They will buy a car next
   week   if _____ .
2. We will stay at home
   tomorrow   if _____ .
3. Henry will pass the
   examination   if _____ .

4. Frank will stay at the office   until _____ .

5. I will wear my new hat
   tomorrow   unless _____ .

6. I will not wear my new hat   if _____ .

7. Helen won't go to the dance   unless _____ .

8. We will eat lunch   as soon as _____ .
9. Mr. Taylor will buy the
   house   as soon as _____ .

10. We will go to the airport   when _____ .

11. I will turn on the fan   when _____ .

12. I will turn it off   if _____ .

Complete the *future action clause* in the following sentences, using a verb in the *future tense*:

13. George will _____ when he gets to New York.

14. He _____ if he has enough money.

15. Helen _____ if John asks her to go with him.

16. We _____ when you come to see us.

17. I will not _____ unless Betty goes, too.

18. We _____ until our guests arrive.

19. Frank _____ as soon as he speaks English well.

20. I _____ as soon as the room gets warm.

21. I _____ when it starts to rain.

22. I _____ when it stops raining.

23. I _____ if I do not find my pen.

Exercise B. In any conditional sentence, the order of the two clauses *may be reversed, placing the "if" clause first.* Answer the following questions, repeating the conditional clause, and *adding a clause in the future tense*:

1. If Henry invites you to dinner, what will you do?

      If Henry invites me ———————————————————— .

2. If Helen has plenty of money, what will she do?

      If ———————————————————————————— .

3. If you decide to go to Alaska, what will you do?

      If ———————————————————————————— .

4. When your brother arrives, what will you do?

      When ——————————————————————————— .

5. As soon as John gets his paycheck, what will he do?

      As soon as ———————————————————————— .

6. If Mr. and Mrs. Green cannot find an apartment, what will they do?

      If ———————————————————————————— .

Idiomatic Use of It Takes

In the idiom "it takes" the verb "take" means to *require* or *necessitate*. Study the following situations to see how the idiom is used:

PRESENT TENSE

      Every day John leaves the house at 8:30 and gets to the office at 9:00.

      It takes John half an hour to get to the office.

          him

PAST TENSE

      Yesterday I wrote the letter in ten minutes.

      It took me ten minutes to write the letter.

FUTURE TENSE

      Helen will finish her work in two hours.

      It will take Helen two hours to finish her work.

          her

This is the order, or the formula, for such sentences:

It takes ⎫
It took ⎬
It will take ⎭

(1)	(2)	(3)
whom? what?	how long?	to do what?

Exercise C.   Write the following sentences, using the idiom *as shown in the model:*

PRESENT TENSE

1. Mr. Jones shaves in ten minutes.

   It takes _____.
2. The maid irons a shirt in 25 minutes.

   It takes _____.
3. I drive to the lake in half an hour.

   _____.

4. We fly to London in five hours.

   _____.

5. A letter reaches Athens in four days.

   _____.

PAST TENSE

6. We flew to London in five hours.

   It took _____.
7. The telegram reached me in two hours.

   It took the telegram _____.
8. I ate my breakfast in 15 minutes.

   _____.

9. She cleaned the apartment in half a day.

   _____.

10. Henry finished the work in two weeks.

    _____.

11. John will paint his car in two days.

    It will take _____.

12. I will eat my lunch in 20 minutes.

    It _____.

13. They will find an apartment in a few days.

    _____

14. Charles will finish his education in four years.

    _____

15. We will get to Hawaii in ten hours.

    _____

This idiom may also be used *without an indirect object*, for example:

> It takes five hours to fly to London.

It may be used *in any tense:*

> It has taken George six days to do the work.

It may be used in the *continuous form* of the verb:

> It is taking Henry a long time to find a job.

Dialog

How long does it take you to eat breakfast?

If I hurry, it takes me less than ten minutes.

I never have time for breakfast, because it takes me an hour to get to the office.

It won't take you an hour if you go with me, because I go on the subway.

LESSON XXX

Tag Questions and Answers—Comparative Clauses, Complete and Shortened Form —Spelling Changes, Doubling the Final Consonant

In some languages, it is customary to use an interrogative "no?" at the end of an affirmative sentence, thereby making it a question. In English, we use the short (or "tag") form shown in the following sentences:

> Charles is your friend, *isn't he* (isn't he your friend)?
> You were not there last night, *were you* (were you there last night)?
> Helen takes music lessons, *doesn't she* (doesn't she take music lessons)?
> Henry has not left yet, *has he* (has he left yet)?

The rules, then, are:

(1) Change the *noun* (if the subject is a noun) to a *pronoun.*

(2) Change from *affirmative* to *negative*, or from *negative* to *affirmative*, using Form 2 or Form 4 from the Verb Chart in Appendix 1.

(3) In the tag question, repeat *only the conjugated part* of the verb. If the first form already contains an auxiliary verb, repeat only the auxiliary. If the first form is Form 1 of the present or past tense, remember that the tag question is *interrogative*, and supply the *corresponding auxiliary*, e.g.: You want a book, *don't you?* He went downtown, *didn't he?*

157

Exercise A. Complete the following sentences with a tag question:

1. Your friend John isn't here today, _____?

2. They have gone to New York, _____?

3. Mr. and Mrs. Miller didn't bring their children, _____?

4. You will not forget to come, _____?

5. The lawyer wrote the letter, _____?

6. He didn't mail it, _____?

7. Mr. Forbes was in Florida last week, _____?

8. I don't have to be there early, _____?*

9. They have to move, _____?*

10. John goes to bed early, _____?

11. He doesn't get up early, _____?

12. You will be there on time, _____?

13. Dick caught a bad cold, _____?

The "tag" answer form is based upon *Rules No. 1 and 3* for the *tag question:*

> Change the *noun* to a *pronoun.*
> Use *only the conjugated form* (the auxiliary) of the interrogative verb; or if the verb is *"be,"* which *does not use an auxiliary* in the present and past tenses, then use the appropriate form of "be."

Were you here yesterday?	Yes, I was.	No, I wasn't.
Did you hear the lecture?	Yes, I did.	No, I didn't.
Were John and Alice with you?	Yes, they were.	No, they weren't.
Do you have to leave now?	Yes, I do.	No, I don't.
Have they left for Europe?	Yes, they have.	No, they haven't.

*Compare these two sentences with the second one. In "They have gone to New York," *have is an auxiliary verb*, and the tag question is *"haven't they?"* In "They have to move," *have is a principal verb*, and the tag question is *"don't they?"*

158

Exercise B. Write "tag" answers to the following questions:

1. Is Henry learning to speak German?

   Yes, _____ . No, _____ .

2. Did they get married last month?

   Yes, _____ . No, _____ .

3. Are they living on State Street?

   Yes, _____ . No, _____ .

4. Have they rented an apartment?

   Yes, _____ . No, _____ .

5. Are you planning to take lessons?

   Yes, _____ . No, _____ .

6. Was Henry studying when you left?

   Yes, _____ . No, _____ .

7. Won't they be here next week?

   Yes, _____ . No, _____ .

8. Didn't you eat before you came?

   Yes, _____ . No, _____ .

9. Weren't you and Tom asleep at seven o'clock?

   Yes, _____ . No, _____ .

10. Is it raining now?

    Yes, _____ . No, _____ .

11. Did the sun shine yesterday?

    Yes, _____ . No, _____ .

12. Haven't you seen that show?

    Yes, _____ . No, _____ .

13. Will you be here tomorrow?

    Yes, _____ . No, _____ .

Comparative Clauses

Study the changes in form commonly used in making comparisons, depending on the meaning intended.

> If I work harder, I will have more money.
>> The harder I work, the more money I will have.
> When John gets more exercise, he feels better.
>> The more exercise John gets, the better he feels.
> When Helen ate more candy, she got (became) fatter.
>> The more candy Helen ate, the fatter she got.
> When I understood John better, I liked him better.
>> The better I understood Jim, the better I liked him.

Exercise C.   Change the following comparisons to the second form:

1. If it rains harder, I must stay here longer.

   The harder _____ .

2. When Frank has more money, he spends it faster.

   The more _____ .

3. When the coffee is hotter, I like it better.

   The _____ .

4. When he smoked more cigarettes, he coughed more.

   _____ .

5. When Robert made more friends, he was happier.

   The more friends _____ .

6. As Philip gets (becomes) older, he understands life better.

   _____ .

A shorter form may be used, *usually* ending with the word "better."

It will be better if only a *few* people come.	The fewer, the better.
7. I hope I can find a *large* apartment.	The _____ , the better.
8. It will be better if you can make a *long* visit.	_____ .
9. It will be better if Tom can find a *cheap* car.	_____ .

10. The lesson must be in *simple*
    form. _____.
11. It will be better if you can finish
    the work *soon*. _____.

Spelling Changes

When we add *ing*, *ed*, *er*, *est*, *ence* (or any suffix beginning with *a vowel*) to a verb or an adjective, we sometimes *double the final consonant:*

sit, sitting
control, controlled
spin, spinner, spinning

hot, hotter, hottest
big, bigger, biggest
occur, occurred, occurrence

Why does this spelling change occur with certain words and not with others? Here is the rule:

Those words which double their final consonant *must end with a single consonant preceded by a single vowel.* They must be words of *one syllable* or with the *accent*, or stress, *on the final syllable.* A few such words are:

ship (shipping, shipped, shipper)
compel (compelling, compelled)
thin (thinner, thinnest)
refer (referred, referring)*

run (runner, running)
sin (sinner, sinning, sinned)
repel (repelled, repelling, repellent)
stun (stunning, stunned)

Why do we *not* double the final consonant in the following words?

sweet, sweeter, sweetest (The final consonant is preceded by *more than one vowel*.)
differ, differed, difference (The stress is *not on the final syllable*.)
form, former, formed (The final consonant is preceded by *another consonant*.)
ship, shipment (The suffix *does not begin with a vowel*.)

The verbs *travel* and *cancel* are sometimes treated as exceptions to this rule. A few people still write: travelling, traveller, cancelled. However, the *preferred* American spelling is: traveling, traveler, canceled.

*We do not apply this rule to "reference" because the *final syllable* in "refer" is *no longer stressed* in "reference."

161

Dialog

Charles found a new job, didn't he?

Yes, and he's getting a much better salary.

Well, the more money he earns now, the sooner he can go to college.

Charles really enjoys working hard, doesn't he?

Yes, the harder he works, the better he likes it.

LESSON XXXI

*The Pluperfect Tense—Sequence of Tenses
—**would rather**—**had better**—Idiomatic Expressions of Quantity and Number: **"a good
deal," "a great many,"** etc.*

Study the *pluperfect* (or past perfect) tense on pages 251 and 256
in Appendix 1. This tense describes something which happened or
existed *before another past action or situation*. It is the *past form* of
the *present perfect* tense.

In a complex sentence (one which consists of an independent plus
a dependent clause), a *past tense in the principal clause* must be followed by some form of *past tense in the dependent clause*. Note the
relationship of tenses in the following sentences:

He *says* he *has found* a
good job.
He *said* he *had found* a
good job.

I *think* they *have been* here
before.
I *thought* they *had been*
here before.

Exercise A. Change the following sentences from the *"present—present
perfect"* combination to the *"past—pluperfect."*

1. I know that John has gone to Argentina.

   I knew that _____.
2. He says that he has not heard the news

   He said _____.
3. I think I have missed the plane.

   _____.

4. Mr. Rogers tells me they have bought a house.

   _____.

5. I hear that you have been sick.

   _____.

6. Elena writes that it has been raining for a week in Merida.

   _____.

7. I know that John has lost his passport.

   _____.

8. Dick tells me that he has had a good time.

   _____.

Exercise B.   Answer the following questions in the pluperfect tense:

1. Had you been in the United
   States before this visit?   Yes, _____.

   No, _____.

2. Had John seen that show before? Yes, _____.

   No, _____.

3. Had you and Charles left
   earlier in the evening?   Yes, _____.

   No, _____.

4. Had the children had their
   breakfast earlier?   Yes, _____.

   No, _____.

Special Idiomatic Forms

   Would rather, followed by the simple form of the verb, may be
substituted for "prefer to." It has the same form in all persons, and
has a *present-tense meaning*.

I prefer to stay here.	= I *would rather stay* here.
Henry prefers to leave now.	= Henry *would rather leave* now.
I prefer **not** to buy it now.	= I *would rather not buy* it now.

164

Note that **would rather** is not followed by "to"—*it is followed by the infinitive without "to,"* which we call the simple form of the verb.

Exercise C. In the following sentences, change "prefer to" to "would rather":

1. They prefer to wait for us.   They would rather wait for us.

2. Helen prefers to watch TV.   Helen _____ .

3. We prefer to live in Miami.   We _____ .
4. She prefers to have the class
   at 1:30.   _____ .

5. I prefer to eat later.   _____ .

6. They prefer **not** to buy it now. _____ .

7. He prefers not to take a taxi.   _____ .
8. John prefers not to work at
   night.   _____ .

9. I prefer not to walk home.   _____ .

Exercise D. Answer the following questions with "would rather," practicing the contractions as indicated:

1. Would you rather stay yere?   Yes, I would (I'd) rather _____ .

   No, I'd rather not _____ .
2. Would Henry rather take the
   boat to Lisbon?   Yes, he'd _____ .

   No, _____ .
3. Would you and Betty rather
   eat downtown?   Yes, we'd _____ .

   No, _____ .
4. Would the children rather have
   milk (than coffee)?   Yes, they'd _____ .

   No, _____ .

Had better, followed by the simple form of the verb, indicates a situation *in the present* in which some action would be preferable to another. It *does not indicate action in the past.*

It would be better for you to stay here.—You had better stay here.*
It would be better for you not to stay here.—You *had better not stay*
here.

Exercise E.   Change the following sentences in order to use "had better,"
practicing the contractions as indicated:

1. It would be better for us to   We had (We'd) better leave
   leave early.   early.
2. It would better for him to go
   away.   He'd better _____.
3. It would be better for them to
   sell their car.   They'd _____.
4. It would be better for me not
   to eat so much.   I'd better not _____.

Exercise F.   Answer the following questions.   Remember that "had
better" is not followed by "to":

1. Had I better leave now?   Yes, you _____.

   No, you _____.

2. Had she better start the work now?   Yes, _____.

   No, _____.

3. Had we better arrive early?   Yes, _____.

   No, _____.

Idiomatic Expressions of Quantity and Number

Learn and practice the following idioms:

a good deal of (a rather† large amount, quite a lot of)   *Singular*
   We had *a good deal of rain* last week.
a good many (a rather† large number of, quite a lot of,
   quite a few)   *Plural*
   There were *a good many clouds* in the sky.

---

*The expression "had better" is not always the exact equivalent of "it would be
better."   It can have a strong cautionary connotation, especially in the negative.

†"*Rather* large" means "*fairly* large" or "*moderately* large."   It indicates some
degree less than "very large."

a great deal of (a large amount, a lot, lots of)   *Singular*
   The jet plane makes *a great deal of noise.*
a great many (a large number, a lot, lots of)   *Plural*
   A great many men were killed in the war.

Exercise G.   Fill in the blanks with the corresponding expression.   Be very careful to distinguish between singular and plural.

1. a rather large amount of time _____

2. quite a lot of trees _____

3. quite a few people _____

4. a rather large amount of money _____

5. a rather large number of books _____

6. a large amount of time _____

7. a lot of trees _____

8. lots of people _____

9. lots of money _____

10. a large number of books _____

Dialog

I'm surprised to see you. John told me you had taken the boat to Bermuda.
No, I thought I'd rather go by plane this time.
Are you going to leave soon?
I'm not sure. I may leave this weekend.
Well, you'd better make your reservation now because sometimes the planes are crowded.

LESSON XXXII

*Conditional Form of Verb—Sequence of Tenses—Possessive Noun or Pronoun Preceded by of—**will** and **would** Expressing Willingness or Desire—**would** Showing Customary Action in the Past*

Study the *conditional form* of the verb on pp. 251 and 256–257 in Appendix 1. The auxiliary verb *would* is the past form of *will*. With reference to *a verb in the past tense*, "would" indicates *future time*.

In the sentence "*He says that he will come*," the future "will come" follows the present "says" in natural sequence. If we change "says" to "said" (*past tense*), we must also change "will" to "would." In the past, then, we say: "*He said that he would come*."

Study the following pairs of sentences, which change from *present* to *past*:

I *think* (that) they *will be* here.	We *know* (that) John *will do* the work.
I *thought* (that) *they would be* here.	We *knew* (that) John *would do* the work.

Exercise A.   Change the following sentences *from present to past*.   Note that the conjunction **that** may be omitted.

PRESENT—FUTURE SEQUENCE	PAST—CONDITIONAL SEQUENCE
1. He *tells* me that he *will do* the work.	He *told* me _____.
2. He *thinks* that I *will pay* the bill.	He *thought* _____.
3. I know that they will arrive on time.	_____.

168

4. They are sure we will rent the apartment. _____.

5. I don't believe Helen will come to the party. _____.

6. Henry says he will go to Canada next month. _____.

7. He tells me he will get married in June. _____.

8. They know that we will pay the bill. _____.

9. I'm not sure that John will finish the work. _____.

10. I think he will have to stay longer. _____.

11. I suppose that Tom will find a good job. _____.

12. I hear that they will stay in London. _____.

Exercise B. The *conditional* form is also used with a stipulation, or "condition," *which is understood*:

1. Would you go (*if you could*)?   Yes, I _____.*   No, I _____.*

2. Would you and John be sorry (*if Henry left town*)?   Yes, we _____.*   No, we _____.*

3. Would Mr. and Mrs. Powers buy the house (*if they had the money*)?   Yes, _____.*   No, _____.*

4. Would they like to live near the beach?   Yes, _____.*   No, _____.*

*Note that the short form, or "tag" answer, would be "Yes, I would"—"No, I wouldn't," etc.

Another Use of the *Possessive Pronoun*:

This is *one of my books*.   This is *a book of mine*.
Paul and Evelyn are *our friends*.   They are *friends of ours*.
Paul is *one of her cousins*.   Paul is *a cousin of hers*.
Mr. Gibbs is *one of our neighbors*. Mr. Gibbs is *a neighbor of ours*.
Mr. and Mrs. Gibbs are *our
    neighbors*.   They are *neighbors of ours*.
Tommy is *one of their children*.   Tommy is *a child of theirs*.

This form may also be used with *possessive nouns:*

I met *one of Mary's cousins*.   I met *a cousin of Mary's*.
Those are *some of Henry's   Those are *some inventions of
    inventions*.   Henry's*.

This form is not very often used with material things, and then only
if the subject possesses several or many of the thing possessed. "A
book of mine" indicates that I have many, or at least several,
books.

Exercise C. Change these phrases, using the new alternate form shown
above.

  1. one of his neighbors   a neighbor of his

  2. one of her friends   _____

  3. one of my mistakes   _____

  4. one of their children   _____

  5. one of her brothers   _____

  6. some of his songs   _____

  7. one of Tolstoy's novels   _____

  8. one of Henry's ideas   _____

  9. one of Helen's sisters   _____

 10. some of our friends   _____

 11. one of Victor Hugo's poems _____

12. one of our hopes   _____

13. some of their relatives   _____

14. some of Goya's paintings   _____

15. one of her dresses   _____

16. some of her letters   _____

17. one of his old sweethearts   _____

Will and Would Indicating *Willingness* **or** *Desire*

Will is the *auxiliary of the future tense,* but it *has another meaning.* In exactly the *same form as the future tense,* **will** may indicate *willingness* or *desire.*

I can cash the check *if you are willing to endorse* it (*if you will endorse* it).

George says that he *does not wish to come* (he *will not come*).

Exercise D.   Rewrite the following sentences, using "will":

1. Mr. Taylor is *not willing to* write the letter.   Mr. Taylor will not _____.

2. Edward *does not wish to* come before eight.   Edward _____.

3. We *are not willing to* sign the contract.   _____.

4. They *do not wish to* sell their car.   _____.

Write the four sentences again, using "*would*" instead of "*will.*" Remember that **would** is the *past form of "will."* This looks like the conditional form here, but it really means "*was not willing*" or "*did not wish to.*"

1a. Mr. Taylor *was not willing to* write the letter.   Mr. Taylor would not _____ _____.

2a. Edward *did not wish to* come before eight.   _____.

3a. We *were not willing to* sign the contract.   _____.

4a. They *did not wish to* sell their car.   _____.

Rewrite the following sentences, using *"will" in the present* and *"would"* in *the past:*

5. I *am not willing to* do that work.

I will not _____.

6. George *was not willing to* take us with him.

George would not _____.

7. Mr. Hall *did not wish to* eat with us.

_____.

8. Mrs. Taylor *does not wish to* travel by plane.

_____.

9. He said that he *was willing to* sign the check.

_____.

10. Henry *does not wish to* accept that job.

_____.

11. Mr. Johnson *was not willing to* go to the meeting.

_____.

12. He *is willing to* pay for the tickets.

_____.

Would Showing Customary Action in the Past

The auxiliary verb **would** is sometimes used to show *customary* or *repeated action in the past*, exactly like "used to." (See Lesson XXIV, page 128). **Would** is frequently *used with an adverb* or *adverbial phrase* such as "often," "always," "usually," "every day," etc.

Study the following examples:

When we lived near the beach, we *often went* swim-
           used to go
           would go
ming early in the morning.

When they visited their grandmother, she *always made*
           used to make
           would make
cookies for them.

Their grandfather *often told* them stories of his
           used to tell
           would tell
childhood.

Exercise E. Rewrite the following sentences, changing the italicized words to "*would*" *plus the verb in simple form.*

1. We *often stopped* to watch the birds.

We would stop _____.

2. He *usually went* to the lake on Sunday.

He would go _____.

3. We *often watched* TV until half-past ten.

_____.

4. We *frequently studied* after supper.

_____.

5. She *always lied* about her age.

_____.

6. He *used to come* late and leave early.

_____.

7. They *used to play* games in the park.

_____.

8. They *often sat* in the park in the evening.

_____.

9. He *often sent* her candy and flowers.

_____.

Dialog

When you were a child, did you use to read very much?

Yes, I read lots of novels. Dickens was a favorite of mine, and I would often stay up late at night reading his stories.

There is one novel of his that I will never forget—the *Tale of Two Cities.*

Would you like to go with me some night to our literary club?

Yes, I'd like very much to go if you would let me know a day or two in advance.

LESSON XXXIII

The Passive Voice—*supposed to*

The *passive voice* is formed with the verb **be** (see Appendix 1, pp. 249 to 253) plus the past participle. You learned about the past participle when you studied the present perfect tense in Lesson XXV, p. 130. If it is necessary for you to find the *past participle of an irregular verb*, turn to pp. 260–261, Appendix 1.

Study the following examples in *four different tenses* of the verb **be**:

ACTIVE FORM	PASSIVE FORM
The students *do* the work.	The work *is done* by the students.
Ruben Dario *wrote* the poem.	The poem *was written* by Ruben Dario.
The police *have found* the money.	The money *has been found* by the police.
The treasurer *will pay* the bill.	The bill *will be paid* by the treasurer.

As you see, the *object in the active form* becomes *the subject in the passive form*, and the *subject in the active form* becomes the *"agent"* in the passive. The preposition **by** introduces the agent in the passive form.

Exercise A. When you change the following sentences to passive form, be sure to follow the verb **be** in Appendix 1, using it in six tenses: present, past, present perfect, pluperfect, future, and conditional. *Do not change the tense* of the original sentence:

ACTIVE FORM	PASSIVE FORM
1. The students *do* the exercises.	The exercises are _____ .
2. Victor Hugo *wrote* the novel.	The novel was _____ .

3. The agent sold the house. _____.
4. Many people saw the accident. _____.

5. Mr. Lee will pay the bill. _____.
6. Everyone will forget the crime. _____.
7. The students learn the new words. _____.
8. The teacher repeats the sentences. _____.
9. The people have chosen a leader. _____.
10. The police have found the money. _____.
11. The thief had hidden the money. _____.
12. A woman had driven the car. _____.

13. Albert would do the work. _____.
14. Miss Taylor would begin the program. _____.
15. Everybody enjoyed the program. _____.
16. Lots of people heard the explosion. _____.
17. The explosion killed five persons. _____.
18. The New York Yankees won the game. _____.
19. The Mayor will meet them at the airport. _____.
20. The manager will send a telegram. _____.

Exercise B. In the following sentences, omit reference to the agent. In other words, omit the phrase "by them," since it is not important.

1. They will do nothing.   Nothing will be done.
2. They have changed their address. _____.

3. They have thrown away their
   money.   _____.

4. They have heard nothing.   _____.
5. They took nothing from the
   house.   _____.

6. They will pay the bill.   _____.

Exercise C. The sentences in this exercise, already in the passive form, will be changed from the simple to the continuous form. You will see on pages 249 and 250 of Appendix 1 that the continuous form of "be" exists only in the present and past tenses. Study Forms 5, 6, and 7 of these two tenses. Then change the following sentences from simple to continuous form, that is, change from Forms 1, 2, and 3 to Forms 5, 6, and 7.

1. Nothing is done.   Nothing is being done.

2. The house is built here.   The house _____.

3. The letter was read.   _____.
4. John was taught by Professor
   White.   _____.
5. The car was driven by a
   woman.   _____.

6. The animals were not fed.   _____.
7. French was not spoken at the
   meeting.   _____.

The Idiomatic Use of "supposed to"

This idiom *takes the form of the passive voice*, and is usually found only in the present and past tenses. It expresses a moderate degree of obligation. Follow its evolution in these sentences:

My mother expects me to get home before eleven.
I am expected (by my mother) to get home before
   eleven.
I am supposed to get home before eleven.

The manager does not require John to work on
   Saturday.
John is not required (by the manager) to work on
   Saturday.

John is not supposed to work on Saturday.*

Alice expected you to meet her at the school.
You were expected (by Alice) to meet her at the school.
You were supposed to meet Alice at the school.

Exercise D. Change the following sentences to express obligation with "supposed to":

1. Henry's friends expect him to pay the bill.
   Henry is supposed to pay the bill.
2. They do not expect me to start the work yet.

   I am not _____.
3. Miss Thompson expects us to wait for her.

   We _____.
4. We expect John to take us in his car.

   _____.
5. We expected John to meet us here. (past tense)

   _____.
6. My friends expected me to be there last night.

   _____.
7. They expected Mr. Miller to make the report.

   _____.
8. We expect Robert to make our reservations for us.

   _____.

Exercise E. "Supposed to" in the same form may express a *belief* on the part of others, instead of an *expectation*.

1. People believe that Mr. Miller   Mr. Miller is supposed to be
   is very rich.   very rich.
2. People believed that she was a   She was supposed to be a great
   great actress.   actress.

*Used in the negative, this expression may have the meaning of "not permitted to":

His doctor told him he was not supposed to eat certain vegetables.

177

3. People believe she has a beautiful voice.

She is _____.

4. People believed they were in love.

They were _____.

5. People believe he has a lot of influence.

_____.

6. People think she is not very clever.

She is not _____.

7. People thought he was a great statesman.

_____.

8. People did not consider him a philosopher.

_____.

Dialog

Was that report written by Mr. Scott?

No, it was written by Miss Lane, and signed by Mr. Scott.

Isn't he supposed to write all the reports?

Yes, he is supposed to write them, but as a matter of fact, most of them are written by Miss Lane or by someone else.

LESSON XXXIV

Should and *ought to*—*Commands and Requests*—*become*

Should and **ought to** followed by the simple form of the verb (the infinitive without "to") express *moderate obligation*.

Exercise A.   Answer the following questions:

1. Should Henry look for another job?

   Yes, he should look for _____.

   No, he should not look for _____.
2. Should I turn on both lights?

   Yes, you _____.

   No, you _____.
3. Should they turn off the air conditioning?

   it

   Yes, _____.

   No, _____.
4. Should Betty leave the money on the desk?

   it

   Yes, _____.

   No, _____.

In the following sentences, we use "ought to" with *exactly the same meaning* as "should":

5. Ought Henry to look for another job?

   Yes, he ought to look for _____.

   No, he ought not to look for _____.

6. Ought I to turn on both lights?

   Yes, you _____.

   No, you _____.

7. Ought they to turn off the air conditioning?

   Yes, _____.

   No, _____.

8. Ought Betty to leave the money on the desk?

   Yes, _____.

   No, _____.

The *past tense* of "should" and "ought to" is formed as follows:

should ⎱
⎰ + have + past participle
ought to ⎰

should have *left*   ought to have *gone*
should not have *left*   ought not to have *gone*

Exercise B.   The following questions are in the *past tense*. Answer them as indicated:

1. Should Henry have looked for another job (last year)?

   Yes, he should have looked for _____.

   No, he should not have looked for _____.

2. Should I have turned on both lights (when I came in)?

   Yes, you _____.

   No, _____.

3. Should they have turned off the air conditioning (last night)?

Yes, _____.

No, _____.

4. Should Betty have left the money on the desk (yesterday)?

Yes, _____.

No, _____.

In the following sentences, use "ought to have" instead of "should have":

5. Ought Henry to have looked for another job (last year)?

Yes, he ought to have looked for _____.

No, he ought not to have looked for _____.

6. Ought I to have turned on both lights (when I came in)?

Yes, _____.

No, _____.

7. Ought they to have turned off the air conditioning (last night)?

Yes, _____.

No, _____.

8. Ought Betty to have left the money on the desk (yesterday)?

Yes, _____.

No, _____.

Exercise C. The following sentences are in affirmative and negative, *present* and *past* forms. Change them from "*should*" to "*ought to*":

1. You should put on your sweater.

You ought to _____.

2. Mrs. Brown should not take off her glasses.

_____.

3. You should call her up tonight.

_____.

181

4. You should have called her up last night. _____.

5. The children should have gone to bed earlier. _____.

6. Henry should not get off the bus here. _____.

7. We should have gotten off at 34th Street. _____.

8. You should not have left your money on the desk. _____.

Change the following sentences from "ought to" to "should":

9. You ought to get on the plane now. You should _____.

10. The children ought not to get up so late. _____.

11. You ought to have gone with us last Sunday. _____.

12. You ought to turn off the fan when you leave. _____.

13. He ought not to take off his coat. _____.

14. They ought to have gotten off at the last stop. _____.

15. You ought to look for a smaller apartment. _____.

16. Frank ought not to have spent so much money. _____.

Commands and Requests

The commands in English are very simple. The *affirmative command* is the simple form of the verb—the infinitive without "to":

Go!   Stay here!   Get off!   Call me up!   Listen to him!
Be quiet!

To give a *negative command*, simply place "don't" or "do not" before the affirmative form:

Don't go.   Do not stay here.   Don't get off.
Don't listen to him.

You may make these commands into *polite requests* by first saying "please," "will you please," or "would you please."

Please be quiet. Will you please call me up.
Would you please sign the letter.

In the case of the *negative command*, when you use "will you please" or "would you please," you *must omit the second auxiliary "do,"* because we *cannot have two auxiliary verbs* in the same clause.

Please don't do* it. Please do not come so early.

Will you please not do it. Would you please not come so early.

Exercise D. Express the following commands in more polite form:

1. Go away! _____ .
2. Don't bother me. _____ .
3. Be quiet! _____ .
4. Turn off the water. _____ .
5. Take off your hat. _____ .
6. Don't listen to them. _____ .
7. Don't turn it on. _____ .
8. Come back before nine. _____ .
9. Give me the bill. _____ .
10. Don't send the telegram. _____ .
11. Don't wait for us. _____ .
12. Look at this. _____ .

Become

Become is composed of two words, *be* and *come*, and literally it means "come to be."

George Washington *became* (came to be) President in 1789.

When used *before an adjective*, **become** is often replaced by **get**:

He often *becomes* tired. (He often *gets* tired.)
She *became* sick. (She *got* sick.)
We *became* accustomed to the noise. (We *got* accustomed to the noise.)

Become of is an idiom which means "happen to." It appears only

*Do is the principal verb in this sentence, and not an auxiliary.

in affirmative *questions (Form 2)*, and never in negative questions (Form 4) nor in answers. It may be used in any tense, though it is not often seen in the present.

What *became of* your
    friend George?
(What *happened to*
    George?)

What *has become of* the
    books they used to
    have?
(What *has happened to*
    the books?)

What *will become of* his
    money after he dies?
(What *will happen* to his
    money?)

The ING-form of **become** (becoming) is used as an *adjective*, meaning "attractive" or "suitable" with reference to some person.

That hat is *becoming to* Betty. (That hat looks nice on
    Betty.)

The suit is not *becoming to* him. (The suit does not
    look well on him.)

Exercise E.   Fill in the blanks with the proper form of *become*:

1. Mr. Fisher _____ treasurer of the company last year.

2. If you _____ tired, you can rest.

3. Olga _____ very nervous when she tried to drive the car.

4. What _____ of the wrist watch you used to wear?

5. What has _____ of all the money they used to have?

6. What will _____ of him if he stops working?

7. Is this suit _____ to me?

8. That color is not _____ to her.

Dialog

I really ought to go downtown today. I am all out of writing paper
    and several other things.

And I am out of envelopes. Please buy some for me if you go to the stationery department.

I'll be glad to. Is there anything else that you need from downtown?

No, thank you. And don't go out of your way to get the envelopes. I should go downtown myself, but I don't have the time.

LESSON XXXV

Future Perfect and Conditional Perfect—
Short Forms to Replace Repetitive Clauses

The **future perfect tense is** not often used in English. In conversation, it can usually be replaced by the *future tense* alone.

Study *Forms 1, 2, and 3* of the *future perfect tense* on pages 252 and 257 in Appendix 1. This tense indicates an action that *will be finished at or before some future time*. The preposition *by*, when it refers to time, means "at or before," or "not later than," and is frequently used with the future perfect tense.

> *by* six o'clock—*at or before* six o'clock
> *by* next week—*not later than* next week

Exercise A.   Answer the questions as indicated:

1. Will Henry have finished the work by four-thirty?

   Yes, he will have finished _____.

   No, he will not have finished _____.
2. Will you and Jerry have had dinner by eight o'clock?

   Yes, _____.

   No, _____.
3. Will the Browns have left by the time we get there?

   Yes, _____.

   No, _____.

The *conditional perfect tense* is frequently used in English, especially in combination with the *pluperfect*. Study the *conditional perfect, Forms 1, 2, and 3,* on pages 252 and 258 in Appendix 1.

Exercise B.

1. Would you have gone (if you had had a car)?
    Yes, I would have gone.
    No, I would not have gone.
2. Would you have told me your age (if I had asked you)?

    Yes, _____.

    No, _____.
3. Would Philip have bought the car (if he had had the money)?

    Yes, _____.

    No, _____.
4. Would Alice have sent me the letter (if she had known my address)?

    Yes, _____.

    No, _____.
5. Would Betty have married Robert (if he had asked her)?

    Yes, _____.

    No, _____.
6. Would you and John have come to the party (if you had received an invitation)?

    Yes, we _____.

    No, _____.

We will have more practice in the use of the conditional perfect when we study conditional sentences in Lesson XXXVII.

Idiomatic Short Forms

In Lesson XIX, page 97, you used the adverb **too** to mean "excessively." **Too** has *more than one meaning*, and in the following exercise it means *"also."*

Study the following models, with their *short forms A and B:*

	FORM A	FORM B
George is happy, and I am happy too.	and I am too.	and so am I.
We went to the show, and they also went.	and they did too.	and so did they.
They were working, and he was working too.	and he was too.	and so was he.
I like coffee, and Helen likes coffee too.	and Helen does too.	and so does Helen.

With the above models, you can form any similar sentence. If the verb is a form of *"be" with no auxiliary before it*, repeat the verb in the second clause in the form that corresponds to the subject of that clause. If the verb is *not "be," and if it has an auxiliary before it, or if it takes an auxiliary in the interrogative and negative forms*, then *use that auxiliary in the short form*. Do not repeat participles or infinitives.

In conversation, you may use either Form A or Form B. In Form B, "so" is used instead of "too," and the order of subject and verb is reversed.

Exercise C. Write Forms A and B after the following sentences:

1. George likes to study, and I like to study too.

   (Form A) <u>and I do too</u> . (Form B) <u>and so do I</u> .

2. I take music lessons, and Mary takes music lessons too.

   _____ . _____ .

3. We bought tickets for the concert, and our friends also bought tickets.

   _____ . _____ .

4. I have seen that movie, and Helen has seen that movie too.

   _____ . _____ .

5. Frank will come to the meeting, and George will come too.

   _____ . _____ .

6. We had heard the news, and they had heard the news too.

   _____ . _____ .

7. Albert is studying hard, and I am studying hard too.

   _____ . _____ .

8. They were here yesterday, and Olga was here yesterday too.

_____ . _____ .

9. I signed the petition, and my friends also signed it.

_____ . _____ .

10. Mr. Taylor has left town, and his brother has left town too.

_____ . _____ .

11. We got off the bus at 18th Street, and Robert got off the bus there too.

_____ . _____ .

12. Robert always gets off at 18th Street, and I always get off there too.

_____ . _____ .

13. The children are very sleepy, and I am very sleepy too.

_____ . _____ .

14. They want to go to bed, and I want to go to bed too.

_____ . _____ .

15. I will get up early tomorrow, and they will get up early too.

_____ . _____ .

The *corresponding negative forms* use "not either" and "neither," with similar use of auxiliary verbs and omission of other words. After "neither," you must be careful to *change from the negative form* of the verb *to the affirmative* (that is, from Form 3 to Form 1). This is because "neither" is a negative word, and *we use only one negative in a clause*—we cannot use "not" in the same clause with "neither."

Study the following examples:

	FORM A	FORM B
Bob is not happy, and I am not happy.	and I'm not either.	and neither am I.
They didn't go to the show, and we didn't go.	and we didn't either.	and neither did we.
I don't like tea, and Tom doesn't like tea.	and Tom doesn't either.	and neither does Tom.

They won't come tomorrow, and Ruth won't come.	and Ruth won't either.	and neither will Ruth.
I haven't seen him, and Karen hasn't seen him.	and Karen hasn't either.	and neither has Karen.

Exercise D.   Write the short forms A and B after the following sentences:

1. George doesn't like to study, and I don't like to study.

   (Form A) and I don't either.   (Form B) and neither do I.

2. I don't take music lessons, and Mary doesn't take music lessons.

   _____ .   _____ .

3. We didn't buy tickets for the concert, and our friends didn't buy tickets.

   _____ .   _____ .

4. I haven't seen that movie, and Helen hasn't seen it.

   _____ .   _____ .

5. Frank will not come to the meeting, and George will not come.

   _____ .   _____ .

6. The children aren't very sleepy, and I'm not very sleepy.

   _____ .   _____ .

7. They don't want to go to bed, and I don't want to go to bed.

   _____ .   _____ .

8. I won't get up early tomorrow, and they won't get up early.

   _____ .   _____ .

9. We had not heard the news, and they had not heard the news.

   _____ .   _____ .

10. Mr. Taylor has not left town, and his brother has not left town.

    _____ .   _____ .

11. We didn't get off the bus at 18th Street, and Robert didn't get off there.

    _____ .   _____ .

12. Robert doesn't usually get off at 18th Street, and I don't usually get off there.

_____ . _____ .

Dialog

Would you have bought that car if you had had the money?

No, the reason why I didn't buy it was that I didn't like it, and neither did my brother.

Well, I prefer the smaller cars, and so does Frank.

I like the smaller cars, too. I would have bought Albert's car if I had known he was going to sell it.

LESSON XXXVI

*Subjunctive Mood—The Subjunctive Used to Express a Hope, Wish, or Command —Present Subjunctive after **suggest, propose,** and Similar Verbs—Past Subjunctive in Conditional Sentences*

The subjunctive is not used so much in English as in some other languages. Perhaps it appears to be used less only because there is so little difference between the subjunctive forms and the indicative forms.

The *subjunctive takes various forms*, and they should be studied carefully on the Verb Chart (Appendix 1, pp. 252–253 and 258–259). The auxiliaries **may, might, let, should,** and **would** are all used to express different shades of meaning in the subjunctive mood. The only difference in form, in the present tense, is that the *present subjunctive* is formed by using the *basic form of the verb* (**be, take, come, go**) *in all persons (without adding "s" in the third person singular).* In the *past subjunctive, only the verb* **be** *shows any difference from the past indicative.*

Exercise A. The subjunctive is used with "may" to express HOPE:

INDICATIVE	SUBJUNCTIVE
1. I hope you will be happy.	May you be happy!
2. I hope he will win the prize.	May he _____!
3. I hope they will come soon.	_____!
4. I hope you will live to be 100.	_____!

192

5. I hope you will have the best
   of luck. _____!
6. I hope he will come back
   safely. _____!
7. I hope your friend will get
   well soon. _____!

Exercise B. The subjunctive may be used with "let" to express a *wish* or *command*:

SUBJUNCTIVE	SUBJUNCTIVE
1. I order that the gates be opened.	Let the gates be opened!
2. I insist that the truth be told.	Let the truth _____!
3. I order that justice be done.	Let _____!
4. I order that all the bills be paid.	Let _____!
5. I insist that the men remain here.	_____!
6. I wish that the laws be obeyed.	_____!

In the same form, the auxiliary "let" is used with the *first person plural* object pronoun to express a *wish*, or a *mild command*, that we do something or that we not do it.

Let us be quiet.   *Let us not* be quiet.

"Let us" is almost always contracted to "let's":

Let's stay here.   *Let's not* stay here.

Exercise C. In the space below, express both affirmatively and negatively the *wish* or *command* that:

1. we leave before
   10:30. Let's _____ . Let's not _____ .
2. we bring Helen
   with us. Let's _____ . Let's not _____ .

3. we buy that house. _____ . _____ .

4. we turn off the fan. _____ . _____ .

5. we wait for George. _____ . _____ .
6. we get on the next
   bus. _____ . _____ .

A subjunctive clause, *always in the present tense*, is used after verbs like **suggest, recommend, insist,** and **propose** (in any tense) to express a wish, suggestion, proposal, order, or recommendation. Such sentences are similar to the first sentences in Exercise B. Here are some examples.

> I believe that George ought to be nominated, and so: I suggest that George be nominated.
> I thought that Frank ought to pay the bill, and so: I insisted that Frank pay the bill.
> (As you see, the *first verb may be present or past*, but *the second verb must be in the present subjunctive*.)

Exercise D. Using the *present subjunctive*, write a sentence which will logically follow the idea expressed in the first sentence. As your principal verb, use *suggest, recommend, propose, order,* or *insist* in the present or the past tense:

1. I thought that they ought to come early, and so:
   I insisted that* they come early.
2. George thought that we ought to have the meeting on Thursday, and so:

   He proposed that* _____ .
3. The doctor believed that Carol should take the medicine, and so:

   He recommended that _____ .
4. I thought that Louise should stay with the children, and so:

   _____ .

5. My friends believe that I should find a better job, and so:

   _____ .

6. I believe that John ought to look for a better job, and so:

   _____ .

---

*The conjunction "that" is not usually omitted in sentences of this type.

7. I think that Mr. Rogers should be nominated for president, and so:

_____ .

8. I thought that Mr. Wilson ought to be Chairman of the Committee, and so:

_____ .

9. Mr. Wilson believed that the meeting should be held on Tuesday, and so:

_____ .

10. They thought that Mr. Evans ought to take care of the money, and so:

_____ .

The Past Subjunctive

Study this form on pages 253 and 259 in Appendix 1, and note that *the past subjunctive is not different in form from the past indicative, with one important exception: the verb "be."* The past subjunctive *is used to indicate something unreal, contrary to fact,* or merely *improbable* or *hypothetical:*

if I *were* king	(but *I am not king*)
if Henry *had* the money	(but *Henry does not have the money*)
if Tom *were* here	(but *Tom is not here*)
if Helen *could* go	(but *she probably cannot go*)

Such clauses form part of the conditional sentences which are called "present unreal," or "present improbable," or "hypothetical." The principal clause of such a sentence takes the conditional form of the verb:

Henry *would buy* the house if he *had* the money.	(He doesn't have the money.)
Tom *would drive* the car if he *were* here.	(He isn't here.)
I *would wear* my new hat if it *stopped* raining.	(It is raining now.)

Exercise E. Complete the following sentences with a *past subjunctive clause*, using the idea suggested in parentheses:

1. Tom would answer the question if _____ .
   (he doesn't know the answer)

2. I would study more if _____ .
   (I don't have much time to study)

3. John would be happier if _____ .
   (he doesn't have a very good job)

4. I wouldn't wear that hat if _____ .
   (but I am not you)

5. I would go to bed early if _____ .
   (but I am not sleepy)

6. They would rent the apartment if

   _____ .
   (it has only one bedroom, and they need two)

Dialog

I just dropped in to say good-bye before you leave. May you have a
   wonderful trip!

Thank you. The doctor recommended that my brother take a rest,
   so we are going by boat.

If I were you, I would forget all about my work and do nothing but
   rest.

That's what we are planning. We're just going to take it easy for a
   while.

LESSON XXXVII

*Review of Conditional Sentences—Exclamations of Admiration and Disapproval—Use of **must** to Express Probability*

You are familiar with the *three types* or *classes* of *conditional sentences* from your practice in Lessons XXIX, XXXV, and XXXVI. Here is a summary of the three classes of conditional sentences, with examples:

Class I: Future Possible (**See Lesson XXIX.**)

FUTURE TENSE		PRESENT TENSE
We *will stay* at home tomorrow	if	it *rains*. (Possibly it will rain.)
Henry *will pass* the examination	if	he *studies*. (Possibly he will study.)

Class II: Present Unreal, Improbable, or Hypothetical (See Lesson XXXVI.)

CONDITIONAL		PAST SUBJUNCTIVE
We *would stay* at home tomorrow	if	it *rained*. (It probably won't rain.)
Henry *would pass* the examination	if	he *studied*. (He doesn't study enough.)

Class III: Past Unreal or Contrary to Fact (See Lesson XXXV.)

CONDITIONAL PERFECT		PLUPERFECT SUBJUNCTIVE*
We *would have stayed* at home yesterday	if	it *had rained*. (It did not rain.)

*The pluperfect subjunctive has the same form as the pluperfect indicative.

Henry *would have*   if   he *had studied.* (He
    passed the   did not study.)
    examination

Exercise A.   Complete the following sentences in Class I:

FUTURE TENSE   PRESENT TENSE

1. George will study in Europe   if __(he has enough money)__ .

2. Mr. Mitchell will do the work   if _____ .

3. My friends will rent the house   if _____ .

4. John will answer the question   if _____ .

5. Eileen will go to the dance   if _____ .

6. I will pay for the tickets   if _____ .

7. Mr. Brent will call the doctor   if _____ .

8. We will take a taxi   if _____ .

Exercise B.   Change the sentences in Exercise A from Class I to Class II, changing only the form of the verbs:

CONDITIONAL   PAST SUBJUNCTIVE

1. George would study in
   Europe   if   __(he had enough money)__ .

2. Mr. Mitchell would do the
   work   if   _____ .

3. My friends _____   if   _____ .

4. John _____   if   _____ .

5. _____   if   _____ .

6. _____ .

7. _____ .

8. _____ .

198

Exercise C. Rewrite the same eight sentences, changing them to Class III:

CONDITIONAL PERFECT		PLUPERFECT SUBJUNCTIVE

1. George *would have studied* in Europe   if   (he had had enough money) .

2. Mr. Mitchell would have done the work   if   _____ .

3. My friends _____   if   _____ .

4. John _____ .

5. _____ .

6. _____ .

7. _____ .

8. _____ .

Exclamations

Exclamations, either favorable or unfavorable, may be expressed by using "*what a*" (*singular*) or "*what*" (*plural*) before a noun. The noun may or may not have an adjective before it.

What a pleasure!   What a shame!   What a man!
What a tall man! What tall men! What nice people!
What a big church! What pretty girls!

If there is *only an adjective*, without a noun, use "*how*" instead of "*what*."

How pleasant! How nice! How terrible!
How interesting! How stupid!

Exercise D. Complete the following exclamations or write an exclamation that is appropriate to the preceding sentence:

1. Our relatives are coming to visit us.   How nice!

2. John is six feet four inches tall.   What a tall man!

3. The lesson is ten pages long.   _____ long lesson!

4. Mr. Brown was killed in an automobile accident.   _____ terrible!

5. Mr. Harrison told us all about his trip. _____ interesting!
6. My aunt paid $29.50 for that hat. _____ expensive hat!
7. Mr. and Mrs. Adams sent me some flowers. _____!
8. George had to walk twenty blocks to his home. _____!
9. The baby is fat and has red cheeks and blue eyes. _____!
10. The mountain is 20,000 feet high. _____!

Must Expressing Probability

The auxiliary verb **must** is commonly used to indicate *probability:*

Mrs. Adams took off her shoes.

Her feet *are probably* tired.
Her feet *must be* tired.

PAST TENSE

Her feet *were probably* tired.
Her feet *must have been* tired.

Mr. Myers didn't go to the meeting.

He *probably isn't* well.
He *must not be* well.

PAST TENSE

He *probably wasn't* well.
He *must not have been* well.

Exercise E. Rewrite the following sentences, using *must* instead of *probably:*

1. It *is probably* raining.   It *must be* raining.
2. He *probably doesn't live* there.   He *must not live* there.
3. They are probably very happy.   They _____.
4. They are probably not very happy.   _____.

200

5. She probably has lots of
   friends.   _____.
6. He probably studies very
   hard.   _____.
7. He probably saves a lot of
   money.   _____.
8. She probably doesn't earn
   much money.   _____.

Exercise F. Following the models for the past tense, rewrite the sentences of Exercise E, changing from *present* to *past:*

1. It *was probably* raining.   It *must have been* raining.
2. He *probably didn't live* there.   He *must not have lived* there.
3. They were probably very
   happy.   They _____.
4. They were probably not very
   happy.   _____.
5. She probably had lots of
   friends.   _____.
6. He probably studied very
   hard.   _____.
7. He probably saved a lot of
   money.   _____.
8. She probably didn't earn
   much money.   _____.

Dialog

Look at those people carrying umbrellas. It must be raining.

You'd better stay inside. If you went out now, you would get wet.

I should have listened to the weather report. If I had known it was going to rain, I would have brought my umbrella.

Look how wet the sidewalks are. It must have been raining for a long time.

LESSON XXXVIII

The ING-form of the Verb—The Idiomatic Use of **got** *with the Verb* **have**

You are familiar with the ING-form of the verb: going, coming, being, taking, studying, etc. This is used in all Forms 5, 6, 7, and 8 in the Verb Chart of Appendix 1. In these forms, it is called the present participle, and its function is that of an adjective.

But the ING-form also functions as a *noun*, and used in this way it is *similar to the infinitive*. In fact, it is sometimes interchangeable with the infinitive:

To see is to believe.   Seeing is believing.

Like the noun, the ING-form may be the subject or the object of a verb, or the object of a preposition. We will consider it first as subject:

Walking is good exercise.   Writing poetry is his hobby.

Exercise A. Complete the following sentences, adding a subject in the ING-form:

1. _____ makes me tired.

2. _____ gives her a headache.

3. _____ is difficult.

4. _____ is easy.

5. _____ doesn't interest me.

6. _____ makes me fat.

7. _____ makes me thin.

8. _____ is a good habit.

The same ING-form is used as the object of certain verbs. Turn back to Lesson XIX, page 94, and review the verb **enjoy**. This verb, and a few others, can take **only** the ING-form as an object.

Exercise B. Answer "Yes" or "No" as indicated:

1. Does Mary *enjoy* playing with the children?

      Yes, _____.

2. Has John *finished* writing the letter?

      No, _____.

3. Has Henry *stopped* smoking?

      Yes, _____.

4. Can't you *avoid* laughing at her?

      No, _____.

5. Can't the child *help* (avoid) stammering?

      No, _____.

6. Would you *consider* trading your car for mine?

      Yes, _____.

7. Would they *consider* renting that house?

      No, _____.

8. Do you *mind** waiting for me?

      No, _____.

9. Would John *mind* lending me his key?

      No, _____.

10. Would they mind paying for the tickets in advance?

      No, _____.

*"Do you mind waiting for me?" means "Do you object to waiting for me?"

A *few verbs* may be followed either by the *infinitive* with "to" *or by the ING-form:*

She *likes* to study.	She likes studying.
He *prefers* to stay at home.	He prefers staying at home.
They *started* to read.	They started reading.
We *began* to sing.	We began singing.
He *continued* to write novels.	He continued writing novels.

Only the ING-form of the verb can be used as the *object of a preposition.* Remember that "to," while it is the sign of the infinitive, *also functions as a preposition:* Do you object *to waiting* for me?

Study the following examples of prepositions followed by the ING-form:

Mrs. Johnson earns her living *by sewing.*
We are interested *in buying* a house.
You must take the medicine *after eating.*

Exercise C.   Answer "Yes" or "No" to the following questions.

1. Did he talk to you *about coming* to the U.S.?   _____.

2. Did he insist *on coming* with you?   _____.

3. Are you interested *in reading* the article?   _____.

4. Is that brush used *for shining* shoes?   _____.

5. Did he sign the check *before leaving* the office?   _____.

6. Did you object *to bringing* him with you?   _____.

7. Does Tom earn more money *by working* at night?   _____.

8. Is James thinking *of getting* married?   _____.

9. Are you accustomed *to getting up* early?   _____.

10. Is Jenny used (accustomed) *to doing* housework?   _____.

204

11. Did Tom get used *to working*
at night? _____ .

12. Can Frank get used *to living*
in a dormitory? _____ .

Exercise D. Complete the following sentences with a verb in the ING-form, plus any other necessary words:

1. Do you always brush your teeth before ___*(going to bed)*___ ?

2. Do you brush them after _____ ?

3. I am glad to know that you have stopped _____ .

4. I am sorry to hear that you have stopped _____ .

5. _____ gives me a good appetite.

6. _____ bores me.

7. Did Mr. Holmes talk to you about _____ ?

8. Does he object to _____ ?

9. It's hard to get used to _____ .

10. They are considering _____ .

11. Would you mind _____ ?

12. The child really can't help _____ .

13. That soap is used for _____ .

14. The artist earns his living by _____ .

15. Mrs. Harris doesn't enjoy _____ .

Many sentences in which the *ING-form is the subject of a verb* may be changed in the following way in order to *use the infinitive:*

INFINITIVE	ING-FORM
It makes me tired *to play tennis.*	*Playing tennis* makes me tired.
It is difficult *to drive in the city.*	*Driving in the city* is difficult.
It is easy *to learn English.*	*Learning English* is easy.
It is interesting *to make new friends.*	*Making new friends* is interesting.

205

Exercise E. Change the following sentences from the infinitive to the ING-form:

1. It is important *to practice* every day.

   Practicing every day is important.

2. It is necessary *to get* enough sleep.

   _____ .

3. It makes me happy *to receive* letters.

   _____ .

4. It is good exercise *to walk* in the country.

   _____ .

5. It is bad for the health *to smoke* too much.

   _____ .

6. It is dangerous *to drive* very fast.

   _____ .

7. It is illegal *to park* your car at a bus stop.

   _____ .

The Idiomatic Use of "got" with the Verb "have"

Some grammarians object to this usage, but it has become very common in the United States and England, and you must be able to understand it when you hear it. It is usually restricted to the *present tense.*

Review the present tense of the verb "have" with the corresponding forms showing the idiomatic use of "got":

AFFIRMATIVE—FORM 1

I have—I've got
you have—you've got
he has—he's got
   she has—she's got
   it has—it's got
we have—we've got
you have—you've got
they have—they've got

INTERROGATIVE—FORM 2

do I have?—have I got?
do you have—have you got?
does he have?—has he got?
   does she have?—has she got?
   does it have?—has it got?
do we have?—have we got?
do you have?—have you got?
do they have?—have they got?

NEGATIVE—FORM 3

I don't have—I haven't got
you don't have—you haven't got
he doesn't have—he hasn't got
   she doesn't have—she hasn't got
   it doesn't have—it hasn't got
we don't have—we haven't got
you don't have—you haven't got
they don't have—they haven't got

Exercise F.   Rewrite the following sentences, substituting the "got" form:

1. *He has* a new car.   *He's got* a new car.

2. I don't have the stamps.   I _____.

3. We have a big garden.   _____.

4. He doesn't have a job.   _____.

5. Do you have a ticket?   _____.

6. He has lots of friends.   _____.

7. We have plenty of room.   _____.

8. Do you have an eraser?   _____.

9. She doesn't have a penny.   _____.
10. Do they have a big
    apartment?   _____.

"Got" may be used in the same way with the *idiom "have to"* (see Lesson XI, p. 53):

> *I have to go* now. = *I've got to go* now.
> *Does he have to sign* it? = *Has he got to sign* it?

The negative is not so frequently used as the other two forms.

Exercise G.   Taking your forms from the models on page 206, rewrite the following sentences, changing "have" to "have got":

1. *I have to find* another job.   *I've got to find* another job.
2. Does he have to go to
   Chicago?   Has he got _____?

3. We have to be there by 6:30.   _____.
4. Do they have to find a baby
   sitter?   _____?

5. He has to get some sleep.   _____.

6. Henry has to get some sleep.   Henry's got _____.
7. The children have to be
   quiet.   The children have got _____.

8. Do we have to stay here? _____?

9. Betty has to leave next week. _____.
10. They have to borrow some
    money. _____.

Dialog

This is a fine day for walking. I always walk to the office, but John
  objects to walking. He prefers riding on the bus.

Walking is very good exercise. I enjoy it when the weather is good.

I can't help thinking that John must be a little lazy since he insists
  on riding instead of walking.

Just a minute. I want to buy a newspaper. Do you mind waiting for
  me while I buy it?

No, I don't mind waiting. Take your time.

LESSON XXXIX

Indirect Speech Patterns in Statements, Questions, Commands, and Requests

A *direct quotation* is one which quotes the *exact words of the speaker*, and it is usually enclosed in *quotation marks* ("....").

If the quotation marks are removed and the words are reported by another speaker, as part of another sentence, the quotation becomes *"indirect."* Study the following models, showing the change from direct to indirect form:

Henry said, "*I don't want to go.*"
    Henry said (*that*) *he didn't want to go.*
Henry said* to me, "*I don't want to go.*"
    Henry told me *he didn't want to go.*
Henry said to me, "*I like your cousin.*"
    Henry told me *he liked my cousin.*
John said to me, "*I will meet you here.*"
    John told me *he would meet me here.*
John said to us, "*I haven't seen her.*"
    John told us that *he hadn't seen her.*
He said to them, "*I can't go with you.*"
    He told them *he couldn't go with them.*

You can see from the preceding models that when you change from a direct to an indirect quotation, you must be sure that the verb of the indirect quotation follows the proper sequence: i.e., *if the first verb is in a past tense*, the *second verb must also be in the past* (past, pluperfect, or conditional); the pronouns in the indirect quo-

*Review the verbs **say** and **tell** in Lesson XXIV, page 126.

tation must correspond to the person or persons indicated in the direct quotation.

Exercise A. Change the following sentences, using indirect quotations. Verb tenses in the direct quotations must be *changed to preserve proper sequence*, and italicized pronouns must be *changed* to preserve the meaning of the sentence:

1. I said to Henry, "I have *your* book."

   I told Henry that I had his book.

2. He said to me, "*I* have met *your* cousin."

   _____.

3. She said to me, "*I* like *your* new suit."

   _____.

4. They said to him, "*We* will go with *you*."

   _____.

5. He said to me, "*I* will write to *you* often."

   _____.

6. John said, "*I* like *my* new job."

   _____.

7. She said to him, "*I* am learning to drive."

   _____.

8. Mr. Johnson said, "*I* will be there early."

   _____.

9. They said to us, "*We* are going to visit *you*."

   _____.

10. Mrs. Brown said to me, "*I* hope *you* can come."

   _____.

Indirect Questions

If the direct quotation is interrogative, in addition to the changes you have already learned to make you must change from the *interrogative form to the declarative:* that is, you must change from Form 2 to Form 1, or from Form 4 to Form 3.

Dick asked me, "*Where did you go?*"
Dick asked me *where I went.*
Ralph asked her, "*Do you have any money?*"
Ralph asked her *if she had any money.*
Henry asked me, "*Will you go with me?*"
Henry asked me *if I would go with him.*
I asked Jim, "*When are you going to leave?*"
I asked Jim *when he was going to leave.*

I asked them, "*What time is it?*"
I asked them *what time it was.*
I asked him, "*Aren't you hungry?*"
I asked him *if he wasn't hungry.*
He asked me, "*Is there a post office nearby?*"
He asked me *if there was a post office nearby.*
She asked him, "*Why don't you buy a car?*"
She asked him *why he didn't buy a car.*

Here are your rules, then, for changing from a *direct* to an *indirect quotation*, when the direct quotation is *a question:*

1. *Preserve sequence of tenses:* If the first verb is in the past, the quoted verbs must be past (past, pluperfect, or conditional).
2. *Watch the pronouns in the indirect quotation:* Remember the meaning of what you are saying as you would have to do in your own language.
3. *Do not use the interrogative form in the indirect quotation.* Change from interrogative to declarative, and if the quotation is not introduced by an interrogative word like *when, where, how, why, who,* or *what,* begin your indirect quotation with *if* or *whether.*

Exercise B. Change from direct quotation to indirect:

1. Jerry asked me, "What *did you see?*"
   Jerry asked me what *I saw.*
2. Helen asked me, "Why don't you call me up?"

   Helen asked me why I didn't _____ .
3. They asked us, "Where do you live?"

   _____ .
4. They asked him, "Do you like the United States?"

   _____ .
5. They asked her, "Don't you want to go with us?"

   _____ .
6. He asked me, "When do you want to leave?"

   _____ .

7. He asked me, "Have you found an apartment?"

   _____.

8. They asked us, "Where is the bus station?"

   _____.

9. I asked him, "Will you go with me?"

   _____.

10. I asked Mr. Tyler, "Are you going to New York?"

    _____.

11. We asked her, "Is it raining?"

    _____.

12. I asked him, "Is there a telephone in your office?"

    _____.

The same changes occur (see p. 211, Rules 1–3) when a direct question is preceded by an expression such as "I don't know," "I'm not sure," "Can you tell me," "Have you found out," "Will you please find out," or *any clause which includes the question as part of the complete sentence and changes it from direct to indirect form:*

What time is it?	I don't know *what time it is.*
Where did they go?	I'm not sure *where they went.*
Why aren't they coming?	Have you found out *why they aren't coming?*
Did they use to live in Boston?	Can you tell me if *they used to live in Boston?*

If the first verb is in the present, future, or present perfect tense, no sequence of tenses is involved. It is *only the past tense* which requires another past tense form in the clause that follows it.

Exercise C.   Complete the following sentences in order to include the question:*

1. When did they arrive?   I don't know _____.

2. When will John be here?   Can you tell me _____.

*None of the sentences in Exercise C requires a change of tense in the indirect question, because any tense may follow the present, present perfect, or future.

3. Have they had their dinner?   I'm not sure _____.
4. Why did Henry leave so
   early?   Have you found out _____?
5. Does he plan to come back
   today?   I'm not sure _____.
6. Where are they going to stay?   I can't find out _____.

7. What is their new address?   I don't know _____.

Commands

When a *command* is *changed from direct* to *indirect* form, it takes the *infinitive with "to":*

> Robert said to me, "Leave your books here."
> Robert told me *to leave* my books there.
> Alice said to him, "Don't call me up."
> Alice told him not *to call* her up.

Exercise D. Rewrite the following sentences, changing the direct command to the indirect form:

1. My mother said to me,   My mother told me to wear
   "Wear your hat."   my hat.
2. The manager said to John,
   "Clean up your deşk."   _____.
3. The officer said to them,
   "Move your car."   _____.
4. He said to them, "Don't
   park on this side."   _____.
5. They said to us, "Bring
   your friends with you."   _____.
6. He said to her, "Stay here
   until I come back."   _____.

Requests

When "please" (or a similar expression) is used with the command form, the *command becomes a request:*

> Indirect *command:* He *told me to come* early.
> Indirect *request:* He *asked me to come* early.

(Review this form with "ask" in Lesson XX, p. 101.)

Exercise E.   Change the following *direct requests* to the *indirect* form.

1. Mrs. Brown *said to me,* "*Please stay* with my children."
    Mrs. Brown *asked me to stay* with her children.
2. Harold said to me, "Please go with me."

    _____.

3. They said to us, "Please visit us soon."

    _____.

4. Mrs. Miller said to her husband, "Please buy the camera for me."

    _____.

5. Mr. Wilson said to me, "Please don't wait for me."

    _____.

6. Alice said to him, "Please don't call me up."

    _____.

Dialog

Henry asked me where he could find a good travel agency.

He must be planning to make a trip.

I really don't know who the best agents are, but I suggested that he ask Mr. Taylor.

Mr. Taylor ought to know where Henry can find a good agency, because he travels a lot.

The manager asked me yesterday if I wanted to take my vacation next month, so maybe I'll be looking for a travel agent, too.

LESSON XL

*Reflexive Pronouns—**have** as Causative—Verbs of Permission and Cause Followed by the Infinitive with or without **to***

Personal Pronouns

I	we
you	you
he, she, it	they

Corresponding Reflexive Pronouns

myself	ourselves
yourself	yourselves
himself, herself, itself, oneself	themselves

Exercise A.   The reflexive pronouns may be used as the *direct object of a verb:*

1. Billy put his hand on the hot iron and burned _____ .

2. Mr. Morris shaves _____ with an electric razor.

3. When I fell down, I hurt _____ .

4. The little girl sees _____ in the mirror.

5. Don't (you) fool _____ . (Slang: Don't kid yourself.)

6. We got off the plane and found _____ in a huge airport.

7. The children hid _____ behind the trees.

8. The automatic motor will start _____.

The reflexive pronouns may be used as the *indirect object of a verb:*

9. When children are alone, they sometimes talk to _____.

10. I often ask _____ that question.

11. She bought a beautiful wristwatch for _____.

12. We bought _____ a watchdog.

The reflexive pronouns may be used as the *object of a preposition:*

13. Helen is old enough now to decide for _____.

14. We discussed the matter among _____.

15. James is self-centered. He likes to talk about _____.

16. Paul and Tom agreed to keep the matter a secret between

_____.

17. You will have to finish the work by _____.

"By yourself" means *alone, without help from anyone,*
e.g.:
He lives *by himself*—He lives *alone.*
She did the work *by herself*—She did the work *without help.*

Exercise B. The reflexive pronouns are also used to give *emphasis* to a *subject noun* or *pronoun.* Used in this way, *two positions* of the reflexive pronoun are possible:

1. I *myself*   I will lead the way *myself* .
   will lead the way.

2. You _____   You must answer the letter
   must answer the letter.
                                  _____ .

3. Mr. Gibbs _____   Mr. Gibbs wrote the report
   wrote the report.
                                  _____ .

4. She _____
   had to clean the rooms.

She had to clean the rooms
_____ .

5. We _____
   moved the refrigerator.

We moved the refrigerator
_____ .

6. You (plural) _____
   invited him.

You invited him _____ .

7. They _____
   had to pay the damages.

They had to pay the damages
_____ .

Exercise C. Complete the following sentences with a *reflexive pronoun* and *any other necessary words:*

1. If you handle that sharp knife, you may

_____ _____ .

2. Marilyn is interested only

_____ _____ .

3. She is very selfish. She buys presents only

_____ _____ .

4. They _____ washed the car. They washed the car

_____ .

5. You _____ must make the report. You must make the

report _____ .

6. Mr. Thompson prefers to live alone. He would rather live

_____ _____ .

7. Alice is very timid. She is afraid to walk home

_____ _____ .

8. Mrs. Ellis has no cook, so she prepares the meals _____ .

9. This machine is not automatic. It does not stop and start

_____ .

10. We do not have a servant, so we cleaned the apartment

_____ .

Have as Causative

Have, followed by a noun or pronoun plus a simple verb, may be used as a *causative*, that is, it may be used to mean "cause to." The following situations and models will show how this is done:

Mr. Hill couldn't paint his house himself, so he got Frank, a house painter, to do it.

> *Active* form, with *have:* Mr. Hill *had Frank paint* his house.
> *Passive* form, with *have:* Mr. Hill *had his house painted* (by Frank).

Robert couldn't clean his own teeth, so he got the dentist to do it.

> Active form: Robert *had the dentist clean* his teeth.
> Passive form: Robert *had his teeth cleaned* (by the dentist).

Exercise D. Rewrite these sentences in both active and passive form, using "have":

1. I can't enlarge the picture myself, so I am going to get the photographer to do it.

   I am going to have _____.

   I am going to have _____.

2. The trousers of Tom's new suit were too long, so he got the tailor to shorten them.

   Tom had _____.

   _____.

3. Mr. Brown didn't write the letter himself; he got the secretary to do it.

   _____.

   _____.

4. Betty can't cut her own hair, so she is going to get Antoine to do it.

   _____.

   _____.

5. Mr. Roberts couldn't tear down the old garage, so he got Tom Carter to do it.

_____ .

_____ .

6. Mrs. Macy cannot wash her windows herself, so she employs Sam to do it.

Mrs. Macy has _____ .

_____ .

Verbs of Permission and Cause

Verbs which express *permission or cause* (like "have" in the preceding exercise) may be classified in two groups:

Class 1—Verbs which require the simple form (the infinitive without "to"):

have	*I had him fix* my car.
let	*I let him drive* my car.
make	*I made him leave* the car here.

Class 2—Verbs which require the complete infinitive, with "to":

ask	I *asked him to do* the work.
tell	He *told me to come* early.
advise	I *advised him to drive* carefully.
allow	She *allowed them to stay* there.
permit	I *permitted John to use* my car.
get	She *got Sam to wash* the windows.
force	The policeman *forced him to stop.*
want	He *wanted me to give* him the key.

Two other verbs, which do not express cause or permission but which take the simple form (without "to") are:

see	I *saw him leave* the house.
hear	I *heard him start* the car.

These two verbs may also be followed by the *present participle:*

I *saw him leaving* the house.
I *heard him starting* the car.

The verb "watch" may be substituted for "see," since it has somewhat the same meaning.

Exercise E. Complete the following sentences with a verb (infinitive *with* or *without* "to") plus other necessary words, being very careful to distinguish between Class 1 and Class 2:

1. I told John _____.

2. He advised me _____.

3. She had the dressmaker _____.

4. We saw Henry _____.

5. Her husband never lets her _____.

6. He sometimes permits her _____.

7. We got a painter _____.

8. We had him _____.

9. Last night I heard you _____.

10. We wanted the children _____.

Dialog

Where can I get my radio fixed? It's out of order, and I can't fix it myself.

Why don't you have Tom Clark fix it? He has a shop on 14th Street, and he does all the repair work himself.

I've had a good deal of trouble with this radio. I don't know whether it can be repaired or not.

Well, take it to Tom and have him look at it. If it can't be fixed, he'll tell you.

LESSON XLI

Nonrestrictive Relative Clauses

Two sentences, when they are *related in subject matter*, can often be combined into one by means of a relative pronoun: **who, whom,* which, whose, when, where.**

(a) I want you to meet Mr. Evans. He lives next door to us.
I want you to meet Mr. Evans, *who* lives next door to us.

(b) This is our classroom. It is the nicest one in the building.
This is our classroom, *which* is the nicest one in the building.

(c) That lady is Miss Taylor. I studied with her last year.
That lady is Miss Taylor, *with whom* I studied last year. (formal)
That lady is Miss Taylor, *whom* I studied *with* last year. (conversational)

(d) We will go the airport at 1:30. Our friends arrive then from Chile.
We will go to the airport at 1:30, *when* our friends arrive from Chile.

(e) They moved to Tulsa. Their parents live there.
They moved to Tulsa, *where* their parents live.

Note that a *comma precedes the relative clause in every case.* Such clauses are called *nonrestrictive relative clauses.*

*See footnote, Lesson XXVIII, page 149.

Exercise A. Rewrite the following, combining the two sentences into one, and using **who, whom, which, when,** or **where,** preceded by a comma. In each case, use one of the above examples as your model:

1. I will spend three days in Boston. My brother is in school there. [Example (e)]

   _____.

2. We would like to meet Mr. Rogers. He teaches biology at the high school. (a)

   _____.

3. The speaker will be Mr. Adams. He was elected President of the Chamber of Commerce. (a)

   _____.

4. That pretty girl is Linda Wills. John is engaged to her. (c)

   _____.

5. They will go to Washington in June. Their son graduates from college then. (d)

   _____.

6. This is Frank Mitchell. I bought a car from him last month. (c)

   _____.

7. That is the new Hotel Hilton. It was built last year. (b)

   _____.

8. I want you to meet Dick Norton. I study with him every night. (c)

   _____.

9. Take a look at this book. I found it at the bookstore yesterday. (b)

   _____.

10. That tall boy is my cousin Tom. I bought the book for him. (c)

    _____.

The relative pronoun _whose_, which shows _possession_, may refer to persons or things.

(a) This is Frank Mitchell, *whose* car I bought last month.
(b) That pretty girl is Linda Wills, *whose* cousin you met at the party.
(c) We saw the Biltmore Theater, *whose* roof was blown off in the storm.

Exercise B. Rewrite the following, combining the two sentences into one, and using **whose**, preceded by a comma:

1. This is Walter Ellis. His car was damaged in the accident.

_____.

2. I want to see Mr. Baker. His wife is in the hospital.

_____.

3. We are going to visit my grandmother. Her birthday is tomorrow.

_____.

4. George is engaged to Thelma Hunter. Her father is president of the bank.

_____.

5. We own stock in the Stanton Hotel Company. Its manager resigned last week.

_____.

6. He belongs to the Chamber of Commerce. Its offices are on the second floor.

_____.

7. This is Mrs. John Anderson. You saw her picture in the paper.

_____.

Sometimes a relative clause may be introduced earlier in the sentence:

Miss Lambert, *who used to teach French at the high school*, has gone to Europe.
This book, *which I found at the library yesterday*, is very interesting.
That pretty girl, *whose name I do not know*, lives next door to us.

Exercise C. Rewrite the following, changing the parenthetical clause to a relative clause:

1. Mr. Jackson (his son was injured in the accident) is a friend of ours.

   _____ .

2. My grandmother (she is 76 years old) lives in a small town.

   _____ .

3. This suit (it just came back from the cleaner's) is a little too small for me.

   _____ .

4. My cousin Tom (I bought the book for him) studies at the University. (See Exercise A, No. 10).

   _____ .

5. The hotel (it is twelve stories high) was built last year.

   _____ .

6. Mr. and Mrs. Morton (they live in Tampa) will visit us next month.

   _____ .

7. Mrs. Foster (her son is an army officer) lives next door to us.

   _____ .

All of the relative clauses which we have studied in this lesson have been "nonrestrictive" clauses, set off from the rest of the sentence by a comma or commas. They are based upon a combination of *two sentences* which are *related in subject matter* but are *independent grammatically*. In the next lesson we will study "restrictive" clauses and see how they are different from the "nonrestrictive" clauses.

Dialog

I want you to meet my friend Don Chapman, whose brother you knew in Panama.

Glad to meet you, Don. I saw a lot of your brother Jim in Panama, where we worked in the same office.

Perhaps you also know Don's cousin Lisa, who was a secretary in that office for several years.

Yes, I think I met her there, but I didn't know her as well as Jim, whom I worked with for a long time.

LESSON XLII

Restrictive Relative Clauses

Sometimes we use the relative pronouns (**who, whom, which, when, where, whose,** and **that**) in a clause which *cannot be placed in a separate sentence* and which is *not separated from the other clause by a comma or commas.* This is called a **restrictive** clause.

> Examples: (a) This is the gentleman who wants to rent the room.
> (b) This is the man whose car I bought.
> (c) Did you see the suit which I bought yesterday?
> (d) That is the girl to whom Henry is engaged.
> (e) We found an apartment that (or which) is large enough for us.

Exercise A. In the following sentences, the first clause is *incomplete in meaning without a relative clause.* Fill in the blanks with the material in parentheses, thus completing the meaning of the sentence:

1. This is the man _____ .
   (He wants to buy our car.)

2. Mrs. Brown is the woman _____ .
   (Her car was stolen.)

3. Tom is the person _____ .
   (I bought the book for him.)

4. This is the apartment _____ .
   (I told you about it.)

5. Here is a belt _____.
      (It matches your coat.)

6. Fred is the mechanic _____.
      (He fixed our car.)

7. Albert is a worker _____.
      (He is always on time.)

8. Jenny is the girl _____.
      (I talked with her yesterday.)

In a restrictive clause, "that" may replace **who, whom,** or **which,** with *one exception: It cannot be used directly following a preposition.*

The relative pronouns **whom, which,** and **that,** when they are used as *the object of the following verb,* or when they are used as the *object of a preposition but do not follow the preposition directly,* may be omitted.

Examples:

(a) This is the man _____.   (He can fix
    (1) who can fix your car.   your car.)
    (2) that can fix your car.

(b) This is the dancer _____.   (We saw her
    (1) whom we saw last night.   last night.)
    (2) that we saw last night.
    (3) we saw last night.

(c) That is the wristwatch _____.   (I like it
    (1) which I like the best.   the best.)
    (2) that I like the best.
    (3) I like the best.

(d) Here is the book _____.   (I was telling
    (1) about which I was telling you.   you about it.)
    (2) which I was telling you about.
    (3) that I was telling you about.
    (4) I was telling you about.

(e) Mr. Thompson is the man _____.   (I work for him.)
    (1) for whom I work.
    (2) whom I work for.

(3) that I work for.
(4) I work for.

Exercise B.   Complete the following sentences with a restrictive relative clause, using the examples on page 227.

RELATIVE PRONOUN AS SUBJECT
See Example (a) and write in *two* ways.

1. This is the clerk _____.   (He made our
   _____.   reservations.)

2. That is the building _____.   (It was sold
   _____.   last week.)

3. I want to see the man _____.   (He signed
   _____.   the check.)

RELATIVE PRONOUN AS OBJECT OF VERB
See Examples (b) and (c) and write in *three* ways.

4. Would you like to see the suit _____?   (I bought
   _____?   it yesterday.)

   _____?

5. Is that the girl _____?   (Richard
   _____?   married her.)

   _____?

6. That is the school _____.   (Paul attends it.)

   _____.

   _____.

228

See Examples (d) and (e) and write in *four ways*.

7. We went to see the show ＿＿＿＿＿＿＿ .   (You told us
    about it.)

    ＿＿＿＿＿＿＿＿＿＿＿＿＿＿ .

    ＿＿＿＿＿＿＿＿＿＿＿＿＿＿ .

    ＿＿＿＿＿＿＿＿＿＿＿＿＿＿ .

8. Is Mr. Taylor the person ＿＿＿＿＿＿ ?   (You addressed the
                                               letter to him.)
    ＿＿＿＿＿＿＿＿＿＿＿＿＿ ?

    ＿＿＿＿＿＿＿＿＿＿＿＿＿ ?

    ＿＿＿＿＿＿＿＿＿＿＿＿＿ ?

9. Betty is the girl ＿＿＿＿＿＿＿＿ .   (He bought the
                                               flowers for her.)
    ＿＿＿＿＿＿＿＿＿＿＿＿＿ .

    ＿＿＿＿＿＿＿＿＿＿＿＿＿ .

    ＿＿＿＿＿＿＿＿＿＿＿＿＿ .

10. This is the pen ＿＿＿＿＿＿＿＿ .   (I can write
                                               best with it.)
    ＿＿＿＿＿＿＿＿＿＿＿＿＿ .

    ＿＿＿＿＿＿＿＿＿＿＿＿＿ .

    ＿＿＿＿＿＿＿＿＿＿＿＿＿ .

11. Is that the course ＿＿＿＿＿＿＿ ?   (Jack is interested
                                               in it.)
    ＿＿＿＿＿＿＿＿＿＿＿＿＿ ?

    ＿＿＿＿＿＿＿＿＿＿＿＿＿ ?

    ＿＿＿＿＿＿＿＿＿＿＿＿＿ ?

12. Thailand is the country _____ .   (He came from it.)

_____ .

_____ .

_____ .

Be very careful never to substitute "what" for "that" as a relative pronoun. "That," as a relative pronoun, means **which, who,** or **whom.**

"What" means **the thing or things which,** and is used in the following way:

> I don't know *what* John said.
> I asked them *what* they were planning to do.
> Tell me *what* you are thinking about.

Exercise C.   In the following sentences, choose the proper word, "what" or "that," and fill in the blanks.

1. He didn't tell me _____ he was going to do.

2. These are the plans _____ we intend to follow.

3. I have never seen the book _____ he wrote.

4. I don't know _____ the title of the book is.

5. These are the books _____ we found in the desk.

6. These books are _____ we found in the desk.

Dialog

Last night we went to see the show that you told us about.
I hope you enjoyed it. The ballet scene was the part that I liked best.
I liked it, too. There were several dancers who performed very well.
I enjoyed the show so much that I think I'll see it again. Perhaps I
  can find someone who would like to go with me.
Maybe I'll go with you. I wouldn't mind seeing it again myself.

LESSON XLIII

Idioms Formed by Verb plus Preposition—Position of Pronoun Object

The following idioms appeared in earlier lessons. All of them end with a preposition:

look at　　　　*listen to*	*wait for*　　　　*look for*
Did you look at the price list?	Yes, I looked *at it*.
Did they listen to the lecture?	No, they didn't listen *to it*.
Will John wait for his friends?	Yes, he will wait *for them*.
Is Henry looking for a new job?	Yes, he is looking *for one*.

The most important rule is: A preposition must be immediately followed by its object. The *object*, either noun or pronoun, *cannot be separated from the preposition*. Sometimes (but not often) the object of the preposition may be omitted, but in that case it remains understood.

PREPOSITION WITH OBJECT	OBJECT OF PREPOSITION OMITTED
Where did you *get on* the bus?	I *got on* at 16th Street.
Are you going to *get off* the bus here?	No, I'm not going to *get off* here.

Speaking of smaller vehicles, for only a few passengers, the idiom is "get in," "get out of."

How many people got in the taxi?	Three people got in.
Where did you get out of the taxi?	I got out* in front of my home.

*Note that when we omit the object, we also omit the preposition "of."

231

In using these verbal idioms, the great difficulty lies in distinguishing between preposition and adverb. Some words are *always prepositions:*

at   for   from   into   of   to   with   without   after

But some other words may be either preposition or adverb:

in   out   on   off   over   up   down   about

How can one know when such a word is a preposition and when it is an adverb? Only by practice. This will be clearer after studying Lesson XLIV and contrasting its idioms with those in this lesson.

Exercise A. Answer the following questions, *repeating the idiom* and changing the noun or noun phrase to a pronoun where such a change is indicated.

1. catch up with—to overtake
   John was half a block ahead of you. Were you able to catch up with him?

   Yes, I was able to _____.
   Charles entered the class late. Did he catch up with *the other students?* (them)

   Yes, he caught _____.

2. feel like—to have an inclination for, to wish to
   Does Henry feel like going out tonight?*

   No, _____.
   Do you feel like taking a walk along the beach?

   Yes, _____.

3. get along with—to live or work harmoniously with, to be compatible
   Does George get along well with *the manager?* (him)

   Yes, he _____.
   Did Helen get along with *the other students?* (them)

   No, she _____.

4. get in touch with—put oneself in contact with
   keep in touch with—maintain contact with

*When a verb is the object of a preposition, it takes the ING-form (Lesson XXXVIII, page 204).

Does Mr. Taylor want to get in touch with the central office?

Yes, _____.

When your brother was out of town, did he keep in touch with you?

Yes, he kept _____.

5. get out of—avoid (usually something one doesn't want to do)
Did Mr. Adams get out of *going to that meeting?* (it)

No, he couldn't _____.

Did he get out of *paying the bill?* (it)

Yes, he got _____.

6. get over—recover from, physically or emotionally
Did it take Frank a long time to get over *his attack of influenza?* (it)

Yes, it took him _____.

Will Mr. Jones ever get over *his son's death?* (it)

No, he will never _____.

7. get rid of—free oneself from
Were you able to get rid of *the mice in your house?* (them)

Yes, we were able _____.

Did Mr. Pratt get rid of *his inefficient secretary?* (her)

Yes, he finally _____.

8. hold on to—to keep in one's grasp
When the wind blew hard, did Helen hold on to *her hat?* (it)

Yes, she _____.

Did you hold on to the railing in order to keep from falling?

Yes, I _____.

9. keep track of—keep a record of, keep oneself informed about
Does John keep track of *his expenses?* (them)

No, _____.

Can you keep track of *all your relatives?* (all of them)

No, _____.

10. let go of—release from one's grasp, take one's hand away from
Should the driver let go of *the steering wheel?* (it)

No, he should never _____.
Does the child let go of his mother's hand when crossing the street?

No, he doesn't _____.
11. look after—take care of
When you leave town, do the neighbors look after *your dog?* (him)

Yes, _____.
Who looks after *the patients in the hospital?* (them)

The nurse _____.
12. look forward to—await with pleasure
Are you looking forward to *your uncle's visit?* (it)

Yes, _____.
Is Frank looking forward to meeting *his cousins in Germany?* (them)

Yes, _____.
13. make up for—compensate for
Did John's later success make up for his previous failure?

Yes, _____.
Does Jane's beautiful voice make up for *her lack of physical beauty?* (it)

Yes, _____.
14. put up with—endure, tolerate
Does the office manager put up with *tardiness?* (it)

No, _____.
Is it hard to put up with *the noise of the city?* (it)

Yes, it is _____.
15. run out of—exhaust one's supply of
Did you stop because you ran out of gas (gasoline)?

Yes, _____.

Did you run out of time before you finished the examination?

Yes, _____ .

16. see about—attend to
Will Charles see about getting *the reservations?* (them)

Yes, _____ .
Will Helen see about *the refreshments for the party?* (them)

Yes, _____ .
Is the plumber going to see about *the leak in your bathroom?* (it)

Yes, he is _____ .

17. take charge of—assume the direction of, assume control of
have charge of, be in charge of—be in control of, be the director
of
Is Mr. White in charge of the office?

Yes, _____ .
When did he take charge of the office?

He _____ three years ago.
How long has he had charge of the office?

He _____ for three years.

18. take hold of—grasp, put one's hand on
Did you take hold of *the electric wire?* (it)

No, _____ .
Did the child take hold of your hand when you crossed the
street?
Yes, _____ .

19. wait on—attend as a servant, serve
Who waited on you at the restaurant last night?

Pierre _____ .
Did that new clerk wait on you at the store yesterday?
Yes, _____ .

These are only a few of the many idioms in the English language. It
is a good idea to buy a book of idioms and try to learn a few every
day.

George has been promoted. He has taken charge of the sales department.

I'm glad to hear it, and I'm sure he'll get along very well in his new job.

Where are you going in such a hurry?

I'm going to the store. I was painting the floor and I ran out of paint.

I'm looking for a quiet apartment. Ours is too noisy and I can't go without sleep.

I hope you find a quiet place. I can't put up with noise either.

How did you get rid of mice at your house?

We got a cat and he got rid of them in a hurry.

I thought everyone had to go to that meeting, but I didn't see you there. How did you get out of going?

I told them that I had to stay at home to look after the children.

LESSON XLIV

*Idioms Formed by Verb plus Adverb or Adjective—Position of Pronoun Object—Idioms with **get**—Intransitive Verbal Idioms —"keep on" Followed by Present Participle*

In the last lesson, *all the idioms ended with a preposition*, and the *object*, in every case, *followed the preposition*. Look again at the idiom "get over": *He will get over it.* **Over** in this case is a *preposition*.

But **over** may also be an *adjective* meaning "finished" or "ended." So, while "get over it" means *recover from it*, "get it over" means *finish it*. Speaking of some task, particularly something disagreeable, we may say "Let's get it over," meaning "Let's finish it so that it will not bother us any longer."

Up and **down** are also words that can be *either preposition* or *adverb*.

PREPOSITION	ADVERB
up the street, up the river	call him up (telephone to him)
down the street, down the river	call him down (reprimand him)

Review the idiom "call up" (Lesson XXIV, p. 124) and the idioms "put on," "take off," "turn on," and "turn off" (Lesson XXVII, pp. 142–143). These idioms end, *not with a preposition*, but with an *adverb*. A noun object may usually follow either the verb or the adverb (or adjective):

Take off *your glasses.*   Take *your glasses* off.

A *pronoun object must follow the verb:*

Take *them* off.

Exercise A. In the following questions, all the idioms end with an adverb or an adjective. Where the noun or noun phrase is italicized, change it to the indicated pronoun, and place it *directly after the verb:*

1. call down—reprimand
    Did the manager call *John* down for negligence? (him)

    Yes, _____ .
    When you failed to stop your car, did the traffic officer call you down?

    Yes, _____ .
2. call off—cancel an event scheduled for the future
    Did they call off *the game* on account of rain? (it)

    Yes, _____ .
    Did the doctor call off *his appointments for Friday?* (them)

    Yes, _____ .
3. carry on—engage in, continue some work or activity
    Who will carry on *the business* after Mr. Evans dies? (it)

    His son-in-law _____ .
    Did George and Betty carry on a long correspondence?

    Yes, they _____ .
4. carry out—fulfill, execute, put into action
    Will the soldiers carry out *the captain's orders?* (them)
    Yes, _____ .
    Are you going to carry out *your plan?* (it)

    Yes, _____ .
5. fill out—complete a form by filling in the blanks
    Do you have to fill out *this application form?* (it)

    Yes, _____ .
    Has Henry filled out *his income tax report?* (it)

    No, _____ .

6. find out*—ascertain, become aware of
Did you find out *the name of the manager?* (it)

No, _____ .

Will you find out *the price of the book* for me? (it)

Certainly, I _____ .

7. give up—surrender, renounce
Will Jack ever give up *smoking?* (it)

No, he will never _____ .

Did the empire finally give up *its colonies?* (them)

Yes, _____ .

8. hold up—to delay; to rob at the point of a gun or other weapon
Did those two men hold up *the bank* yesterday? (it)

Yes, _____ .

Did the fire hold up traffic on Main Street?

Yes, _____ .

9. look up—to search for something in a list, like a directory or dictionary
Do you always look up *the new words* in your dictionary? (them)

Yes, _____ .

Will you look up *Jane's number* in the telephone book? (it)

Yes, _____ .

10. make up—to improvise or invent
Did the child make up *that fantastic story?* (it)

Yes, he _____ .

Did Susan make up *the words for the school song?* (them)

Yes, she _____ .

*"Find out" ends with an adverb, but "find out *about*" ends with a preposition, like the idioms in Lesson XLIII. Compare:

> He didn't *find it out*. (adverb)
> He didn't *find out about it*. (preposition)

239

11. pick out—to choose, select
Does Mr. Jones pick out *his wife's hats?* (them)

No, _____.
Who picked out *the furniture for their apartment?* (it)

Mrs. Jones _____.
12. put off—to postpone
Are Helen and Robert going to put off *their wedding?* (it)

No, _____.
Did the secretary put off *writing the letter?* (it)

Yes, she _____.
13. put out—to extinguish, as a fire or a light
Does the watchman always put out *the lights?* (them)

Yes, he always _____.
Can the firemen put out *the fire?* (it)

Yes, _____.
14. see off—to accompany a traveler to his point of departure
Did you go to the airport to see *Helen* off? (her)

Yes, _____.
Did he go to the railway station to see *his friends* off? (them)

Yes, _____.
15. try on—to put on a garment, jewelry, etc., in order to test its size or appearance
Would you like to try on *the coat* before buying it? (it)

Yes, _____.
Did you try on *the shoes* before you bought them? (them)

Yes, _____.
16. turn down—to decline or dismiss; to lessen the volume of sound
Will you have to turn down *the invitation?* (it)

Yes, _____.
Did Betty turn down *John's proposal?* (it)

Yes, _____.

Did Betty turn *John* down? (him)

Yes, _____ .

Will you turn down the *radio?* (it)

Yes, _____ .

Idioms with *get* and Other Intransitive Verbal Idioms

The verb **get** is used in many idioms. It can mean "to arrive," as in *get home, get back, get there*; or it can mean "to become," as in *get sick, get well, get cold, get warm, get tired*, etc. *These idioms do not take an object.*

A number of other similar idioms (verb plus adverb or adjective) are *intransitive*, that is, *they do not take an object.* For example:

> *give out, run out*—to become exhausted, as a supply of water, food, etc.
> (Compare with "run out of"—Lesson XLIII, pp. 234–235, No. 15.)
> Their supply of water *gave out*, and they became very thirsty.
> The sandwiches *ran out* before the party was over.

> *go off*—to explode or make a sudden loud noise
> The gun *went off* accidentally.
> My alarm clock *didn't go off* this morning, and I overslept.

> *go out*—to stop burning or shining
> The lights *went out* all over the city.
> The fire *has* not *gone out* yet.

Keep on Followed by Present Participle

The idiom *keep on* followed by the present participle (an ING-form of the verb) does not belong to any of the preceding categories. It means "to continue without stopping." It should be memorized and practiced because it is quite commonly used in English:

> The child *kept on* crying. (The child continued to cry.)
> It *kept on* raining all night. (It continued to rain all night.)
> The two women *kept on* talking over the telephone. (They continued to talk.)

Five Short Dialogs

Why did you put off buying the suit?
Because I want to try it on first, and I don't have time for that today.

I'm sorry to be late. My alarm clock didn't go off.
That's all right. I was late too, because traffic was held up for half an hour on Main Street.

Did Phil turn down that job as assistant office manager?
Yes, he thought he would be better off in the sales department.

How can I find out where John lives?
He has a telephone, and you can look up his address in the telephone directory.

Do you know why they called off the meeting?
I think it was because all the lights in the building went out.

LESSON XLV

Idiomatic Use of **matter**—*whenever, wherever, whichever, whatever, whoever*—*Emphatic Form of Verb*—*Some Common Idioms*

The word **matter** has several different meanings, but in this lesson we are concerned only with its use in two common English idioms: *What's the matter?* and *It doesn't matter.*

When used as a noun, preceded by "the," **matter** can mean a *difficulty*, a *source of trouble*, a *condition which requires a remedy*. Within the sentence, we can substitute the adjective "wrong" for the words "the matter":

> What is *wrong* with your car?—What is *the matter* with your car?
> John looks sick; what is *wrong* with him?—What's *the matter* with him?

The question may also take this form:

> Is anything *the matter* with him?   Is something *the matter* with it?

Such questions may be answered specifically.

> John has a bad cold. The car is out of order.

Or they may be answered by repeating the word **matter:**

> There is something *the matter* with him.
> There is nothing *the matter* with him.

> Something is *the matter* with it.
> Nothing is *the matter* with it.

Exercise A. Taking your models from the above examples, rewrite the following sentences, substituting "the matter" for "wrong":

1. Is something *wrong* with the telephone?

   Is something *the matter* _____?

2. What is wrong with his radio?

   What's _____?

3. You don't look well; what is wrong with you?

   _____.

4. There's nothing wrong with this pen.

   _____.

5. Something is wrong with this typewriter.

   _____.

6. There is something wrong with the TV set.

   _____.

As a *verb*, **matter** means "to be of importance." With this meaning it is used principally in *negative* and *interrogative* sentences.

We may say "How much money he has is not important" or "It is not important how much money he has."

Changing to the verb **matter**, we say:

It doesn't matter how much money he has.

The interrogative form of the sentence would be:

Does it matter how much money he has? (Is it important?)

Exercise B. Rewrite the following sentences, changing them to the negative "It doesn't matter":

1. *Where* they live is not important.

   It doesn't matter *where* _____.

2. *What* she said is not important.

   It _____.

3. It isn't important *when* he gets back.

   It _____.

4. It isn't important *who* signed the letter.

   It _____.

5. *Why* he went away is not important.

   It _____.

Change the above five sentences to the interrogative form:

6. Is it important *where* they live?

   Does it matter *where* they live?

7. Is it important *what* she
   said?   _____?
8. Is it important *when* he
   gets back?   _____?
9. Is it important *who* signed
   the letter?   _____?
10. Is it important *why* he went
    away?   _____?

The phrase "no matter" means "It doesn't matter" or "It is of no importance," but it may introduce a *dependent clause*, in which case *another clause must be added* to make a complete sentence:

(a) *No matter how* much money he has, she will not marry him.
(b) *No matter where* they live, I will go to visit them.
(c) *No matter who* signed the letter, it will be read with interest.
(d) *No matter what* she says, I believe her.
(e) *No matter which* road you take, you will reach the lakeshore.

Whenever, Wherever, Whoever, Whatever, Whichever

The adverbs **whenever** and **wherever** can replace "no matter when" and "no matter where," respectively. Like "no matter," these adverbs introduce a *dependent clause:*

Whenever they come, they will be welcome.
Wherever they live, I will go to visit them.

The pronouns **whoever, whatever,** and **whichever** can replace "no matter who," "no matter what," and "no matter which." They are used as part of a clause which may be the *subject* or the *object* of the principal verb, or the object of a preposition, in a complete sentence:

(a) *Whatever* you do will be all right. (meaning: "anything that you do")
(b) He will buy *whatever* his wife wants.
(c) *Whichever* road you take will lead you to the park.
(d) *Whoever* wrote the letter does not know how to spell.
(e) A reward will be paid to *whoever* finds the money.

Exercise C. Fill in the blanks in the following sentences with *whenever, wherever, whoever, whatever,* or *whichever:*

1. _____ you want to go to the airport, I will call a taxi.

2. _____ she goes, he will follow her.

3. _____ finds the money will get a reward.

4. He believes _____ she says.

5. I will buy _____ hat (of two hats) you like best.

6. _____ they tell you, don't believe them.

7. I will be here _____ they arrive.

The Emphatic Form of the Verb

Emphasis is most often a matter of intonation. In a negative sentence, for instance, emphasis is given to the verb by *stressing* the word "not":

> I am *not* going to the meeting.
> He does *not* want to come.

When the verb is affirmative, and an auxiliary is used, the verb may be emphasized by *stressing* the *auxiliary:*

> Yes, he *can* speak German.
> Yes, I *have* seen that show.
> Yes, they *will* pay the bill.

Since in the present and past tenses the affirmative form (Form 1) does not have an auxiliary, we may, in order to give emphasis to the verb, *add the auxiliary used in Forms 2 and 3:* do, does, or did.

> Yes, I *do* want to see that show.
> Yes, he *does* feel better today.
> Yes, they *did* come to see us.
> Yes, she *did* work in that office.

Exercise D. Change the following affirmative sentences to the emphatic form by adding an auxiliary verb (*do* or *does* in the present tense, *did* in the past):

1. I want to come back
   tomorrow.   I *do* want to come back
                                  tomorrow.

2. He lives on Tenth Street.   _____.

3. She works at the bank.   _____.

4. We have some spare time.   _____.

5. They intend to buy tickets.   _____.

6. They intended to buy tickets. _____.

7. She worked at the bank.   _____.

8. We had some spare time.   _____.

9. I wanted to come back
   yesterday.   _____.

10. He lived on Tenth Street.   _____.

Some Common Idioms

In Lessons XLIII and XLIV there are examples of only a few of the many idioms that are used in the English language. A few more common idioms, which do not involve verbs and their objects, are given below, with sentences to be practiced orally:

1. *all right*—satisfactory, correct, in good order, "O.K."
   The car was out of order, but it is *all right* now.
   What John said was *all right*.
   Please put this book away for me. *All right*, I will.
2. *at all*—in any way (not at all—not in the least)
   He has no money *at all*.
   She doesn't speak French *at all*.
   Are you tired? Not *at all*.
3. *at once, right away*—immediately
   Can you do this for me *at once*? Yes, I will do it *right away*.
4. *for good*—permanently
   Mr. and Mrs. Miller have left town *for good*. (They will not come back.)
   Their son is coming back to town *for good*. (He will stay in town.)

5. *on purpose*—intentionally

He set fire to the building *on purpose*.

She left the window open *on purpose*.

6. *to be through*, *to get through*—to finish (with personal subject)

He *was through* (with his work) before five o'clock.

I left when I *got through* (with my work).

7. *to be over*—to be ended, finished (with impersonal subject)

The meeting *was over* at nine o'clock.

After the class *was over*, they went to the coffee shop.

8. *to be up*—finished, ended, with reference to time

I can't leave before the time *is up*.

He stayed in prison until his time *was up*.

9. *off*—in circumstances, especially with regard to material welfare

well off: The Millers have plenty of money; they are very *well off*.

better off: Mr. Adams is very sick, and he wants to stay at home; but he would be *better off* in a hospital.

worse off: He moved to another city, but found that he was *worse off* than before.

10. *never mind*—don't be concerned (always a negative command)

Did you lose your dog? *Never mind*—he will come back.

Is Frank angry with you? *Never mind*—he will get over it.

Dialog

What's the matter with your telephone? I tried to call you, but the line was always busy.

There's nothing the matter with the phone. It's my teen-age sister. Whenever she gets on the line she goes on talking for hours.

Well, I really did want to talk with you last night after we got through with our meeting.

I guess I'll have to put a ten-minute limit on my sister's conversations and see that she stops when the time is up.

That's a good idea. You don't want to miss an important call.

APPENDIX I

VERB CHART

KEY TO FORM NUMBERS:

Simple Form	Continuous Form
1. Affirmative	5. Affirmative
2. Interrogative	6. Interrogative
3. Negative	7. Negative
4. Negative Interrogative	8. Negative Interrogative

THE VERB *BE*

Infinitive: to be Past tense: was, were Past Participle: been
Present Participle: being

PRESENT

1. I am
   you are
   he is, she is, it is
   we are
   you are
   they are

2. am I?
   are you?
   is he? is she? is it?
   are we?
   are you?
   are they?

3. I am not
   you are not
   he is not, she is not, it is not
   we are not
   you are not
   they are not

4. am I not?
   aren't you?
   isn't he? isn't she? isn't it?
   aren't we?
   aren't you?
   aren't they?

5. I am being
   you are being
   he is being
   we are being
   you are being
   they are being

6. am I being?
   are you being?
   is he being?
   are we being?
   are you being?
   are they being?

7. I am not being
    you are not being
    he is not being[1]
    we are not being
    you are not being
    they are not being

8. am I not being?
    aren't you being?
    isn't he being?
    aren't we being?
    aren't you being?
    aren't they being?

PAST

1. I was
    you were
    he was, she was
    we were
    you were
    they were

2. was I?
    were you?
    was he? was she?
    were we?
    were you?
    were they?

3. I was not
    you were not
    he was not
    we were not
    you were not
    they were not

4. wasn't I?
    weren't you?
    wasn't he?
    weren't we?
    weren't you?
    weren't they?

5. I was being
    you were being
    he was being[1]
    we were being
    you were being
    they were being

6. was I being?
    were you being?
    was he being?
    were we being?
    were you being?
    were they being?

7. I was not being
    you were not being
    he was not being
    we were not being
    you were not being
    they were not being

8. wasn't I being?
    weren't you being?
    wasn't he being?
    weren't we being?
    weren't you being?
    weren't they being?

FUTURE[2]

1. I will be
    you will be
    he will be
    we will be
    you will be
    they will be

2. will I be?
    will you be?
    will he be?
    will we be?
    will you be?
    will they be?

3. I will not be
    you will not be

4. won't I be?
    won't you be?

[1] The 3d person singular always includes three pronouns: *he*, *she*, and *it*. For reasons of space, the second and third pronouns are sometimes omitted in this chart.

[2] Note: The continuous forms (Forms 5, 6, 7, and 8) are not used in this tense of the verb "be."

he will not be   won't he be?
we will not be   won't we be?
you will not be   won't you be?
they will not be   won't they be?

PRESENT PERFECT[1]

1. I have been
   you have been
   he has been
   we have been
   you have been
   they have been

2. have I been?
   have you been?
   has he been?
   have we been?
   have you been?
   have they been?

3. I have not been
   you have not been
   he has not been
   we have not been
   you have not been
   they have not been

4. haven't I been?
   haven't you been?
   hasn't he been?
   haven't we been?
   haven't you been?
   haven't they been?

PLUPERFECT (PAST PERFECT)[1]

1. I had been
   you had been
   he had been
   we had been
   you had been
   they had been

2. had I been?
   had you been?
   had he been?
   had we been?
   had you been?
   had they been?

3. I had not been
   you had not been
   he had not been
   we had not been
   you had not been
   they had not been

4. hadn't I been?
   hadn't you been?
   hadn't he been?
   hadn't we been?
   hadn't you been?
   hadn't they been?

CONDITIONAL[1]

1. I would be
   you would be
   he would be
   we would be
   you would be
   they would be

2. would I be?
   would you be?
   would he be?
   would we be?
   would you be?
   would they be?

3. I would not be
   you would not be
   he would not be
   we would not be
   you would not be
   they would not be

4. wouldn't I be?
   wouldn't you be?
   wouldn't he be?
   wouldn't we be?
   wouldn't you be?
   wouldn't they be?

[1]Note: The continuous forms (Forms 5, 6, 7, and 8) are not used in these tenses of the verb "be."

FUTURE PERFECT[1]

1. I will have been
   you will have been
   he will have been
   we will have been
   you will have been
   they will have been

2. will I have been?
   will you have been?
   will he have been?
   will we have been?
   will you have been?
   will they have been?

3. I will not have been
   you will not have been
   he will not have been
   we will not have been
   you will not have been
   they will not have been

4. won't I have been?
   won't you have been?
   won't he have been?
   won't we have been?
   won't you have been?
   won't they have been?

CONDITIONAL PERFECT[1]

1. I would have been
   you would have been
   he would have been
   we would have been
   you would have been
   they would have been

2. would I have been?
   would you have been?
   would he have been?
   would we have been?
   would you have been?
   would they have been?

3. I would not have been
   you would not have been
   he would not have been
   we would not have been
   you would not have been
   they would not have been

4. wouldn't I have been?
   wouldn't you have been?
   wouldn't he have been?
   wouldn't we have been?
   wouldn't you have been?
   wouldn't they have been?

SUBJUNCTIVE MOOD

PRESENT*

The present tense has various forms, such as the following:

Affirmative	*Negative*
I be	I not be
you be	you not be
he be	he not be
we be	we not be

---

*In certain constructions, the present subjunctive may be expressed with the auxiliaries "should" and "might." Such usage must be learned in practice, with complete sentence models.

---

[1]Note: The continuous forms (Forms 5, 6, 7, and 8) are not used in these tenses of the verb "be."

you be
they be

Affirmative
may I be
may you be
may he be
may we be
may you be
may they be

Affirmative
let me be
. . . .
let him be
let us be
   (let's be)
let them be

you not be
they not be

Negative
may I not be
may you not be
may he not be
may we not be
may you not be
may they not be

Negative
let me not be
. . . .
let him not be
let us not be
   (let's not be)
let them not be

Past*

Affirmative
I were
you were
he were
we were
you were
they were

Negative
I were not
you were not
he were not
we were not
you were not
they were not

All of the other tenses are the same in the subjunctive mood as in the indicative.

IMPERATIVE MOOD

Affirmative
Be

Negative
Do not be (Don't be)

THE VERB *WORK*

Infinitive: to work

Past Tense: worked

Past Participle: worked

Present Participle: working

*The verb "be" is the only verb that has a distinct form in the past subjunctive. Like the present subjunctive, the past may be expressed by using the auxiliaries "should" and "might."

1. I work
   you work
   he works, she works,
      it works
   we work
   you work
   they work

2. do I work?
   do you work?
   does he work? does she
      work? does it work?
   do we work?
   do you work?
   do they work?

3. I do not work
   you do not work
   he does not work
      she does not work
   we do not work
   you do not work
   they do not work

4. don't I work?
   don't you work?
   doesn't he work?
      doesn't she work?
   don't we work?
   don't you work?
   don't they work?

5. I am working
   you are working
   he is working
   we are working
   you are working
   they are working

6. am I working?
   are you working?
   is he working?
   are we working?
   are you working?
   are they working?

7. I am not working
   you are not working
   he is not working
   we are not working
   you are not working
   they are not working

8. am I not working?
   aren't you working?
   isn't he working?
   aren't we working?
   aren't you working?
   aren't they working?

PAST

1. I worked
   you worked
   he worked
   we worked
   you worked
   they worked

2. did I work?
   did you work?
   did he work?
   did we work?
   did you work?
   did they work?

3. I did not work
   you did not work
   he did not work
   we did not work
   you did not work
   they did not work

4. didn't I work?
   didn't you work?
   didn't he work?
   didn't we work?
   didn't you work?
   didn't they work?

5. I was working
   you were working
   he was working
   we were working

6. was I working?
   were you working?
   was he working?
   were we working?

you were working
they were working

were you working?
were they working?

7. I was not working
you were not working
he was not working
we were not working
you were not working
they were not working

8. wasn't I working?
weren't you working?
wasn't he working?
weren't we working?
weren't you working?
weren't they working?

FUTURE

1. I will work
you will work
he will work
we will work
you will work
they will work

2. will I work?
will you work?
will he work?
will we work?
will you work?
will they work?

3. I will not work
you will not work
he will not work
we will not work
you will not work
they will not work

4. won't I work?
won't you work?
won't he work?
won't we work?
won't you work?
won't they work?

5. I will be working
you will be working
he will be working
we will be working
you will be working
they will be working

6. will I be working?
will you be working?
will he be working?
will we be working?
will you be working?
will they be working?

7. I will not be working
you will not be working
he will not be working
we will not be working
you will not be working
they will not be working

8. won't I be working?
won't you be working?
won't he be working?
won't we be working?
won't you be working?
won't they be working?

PRESENT PERFECT

1. I have worked
you have worked
he has worked
we have worked
you have worked
they have worked

2. have I worked?
have you worked?
has he worked?
have we worked?
have you worked?
have they worked?

3. I have not worked
you have not worked
he has not worked
we have not worked

4. haven't I worked?
haven't you worked?
hasn't he worked?
haven't we worked?

you have not worked
they have not worked

haven't you worked?
haven't they worked?

5. I have been working
you have been working
he has been working
we have been working
you have been working
they have been working

6. have I been working?
have you been working?
has he been working?
have we been working?
have you been working?
have they been working?

7. I have not been working
you have not been working
he has not been working
we have not been working
you have not been working
they have not been working

8. haven't I been working?
haven't you been working?
hasn't he been working?
haven't we been working?
haven't you been working?
haven't they been working?

PLUPERFECT (PAST PERFECT)

1. I had worked
you had worked
he had worked
we had worked
you had worked
they had worked

2. had I worked?
had you worked?
had he worked?
had we worked?
had you worked?
had they worked?

3. I had not worked
you had not worked
he had not worked
we had not worked
you had not worked
they had not worked

4. hadn't I worked?
hadn't you worked?
hadn't he worked?
hadn't we worked?
hadn't you worked?
hadn't they worked?

5. I had been working
you had been working
he had been working
we had been working
you had been working
they had been working

6. had I been working?
had you been working?
had he been working?
had we been working?
had you been working?
had they been working?

7. I had not been working
you had not been working
he had not been working
we had not been working
you had not been working
they had not been working

8. hadn't I been working?
hadn't you been working?
hadn't he been working?
hadn't we been working?
hadn't you been working?
hadn't they been working?

CONDITIONAL

1. I would work
you would work
he would work
we would work

2. would I work?
would you work?
would he work?
would we work?

you would work
they would work

would you work?
would they work?

3. I would not work
you would not work
he would not work
we would not work
you would not work
they would not work

4. wouldn't I work?
wouldn't you work?
wouldn't he work?
wouldn't we work?
wouldn't you work?
wouldn't they work?

5. I would be working
you would be working
he would be working
we would be working
you would be working
they would be working

6. would I be working?
would you be working?
would he be working?
would we be working?
would you be working?
would they be working?

7. I would not be working
you would not be working
he would not be working
we would not be working
you would not be working
they would not be working

8. wouldn't I be working?
wouldn't you be working?
wouldn't he be working?
wouldn't we be working?
wouldn't you be working?
wouldn't they be working?

Future Perfect

1. I will have worked
you will have worked
he will have worked
we will have worked
you will have worked
they will have worked

2. will I have worked?
will you have worked?
will he have worked?
will we have worked?
will you have worked?
will they have worked?

3. I will not have worked
you will not have worked
he will not have worked
we will not have worked
you will not have worked
they will not have worked

4. won't I have worked?
won't you have worked?
won't he have worked?
won't we have worked?
won't you have worked?
won't they have worked?

5. I will have been working
you will have been working
he will have been working
we will have been working
you will have been working
they will have been working

6. will I have been working?
will you have been working?
will he have been working?
will we have been working?
will you have been working?
will they have been working?

7. I will not have been working
you will not have been working
he will not have been working
we will not have been working
you will not have been working
they will not have been working

8. won't I have been working?
won't you have been working?
won't he have been working?
won't we have been working?
won't you have been working?
won't they have been working?

1. I would have worked
   you would have worked
   he would have worked
   we would have worked
   you would have worked
   they would have worked

2. would I have worked?
   would you have worked?
   would he have worked?
   would we have worked?
   would you have worked?
   would they have worked?

3. I would not have worked
   you would not have worked
   he would not have worked
   we would not have worked
   you would not have worked
   they would not have worked

4. wouldn't I have worked?
   wouldn't you have worked?
   wouldn't he have worked?
   wouldn't we have worked?
   wouldn't you have worked?
   wouldn't they have worked?

5. I would have been working
   you would have been working
   he would have been working
   we would have been working
   you would have been working
   they would have been working

6. would I have been working?
   would you have been working?
   would he have been working?
   would we have been working?
   would you have been working?
   would they have been working?

7. I would not have been working
   you would not have been
     working
   he would not have been working
   we would not have been working
   you would not have been
     working
   they would not have been
     working

8. wouldn't I have been working?

   wouldn't you have been working?
   wouldn't he have been working?
   wouldn't we have been working?

   wouldn't you have been working?
   wouldn't they have been
     working?

SUBJUNCTIVE MOOD

PRESENT*

The present tense has various forms, such as the following:

Affirmative
I work
you work
he work, she work,
  it work
we work

Negative
I not work
you not work
he not work, she not
  work, it hot work
we not work

---

*In certain constructions, the present subjunctive may be expressed with the auxiliary verbs "should" and "might." Such usage must be learned in practice, with complete sentence models.

you work
they work

Affirmative
let me work

. . . .

let him work
let her (it) work
let us work
(let's work)

. . . .

let them work

Affirmative
may I work
may you work
may he work, may she
    work, may it work
may we work
may you work
may they work

you not work
they not work

Negative
let me not work

. . . .

let him not work
let her (it) not work
let us not work
(let's not work)

. . . .

let them not work

Negative
may I not work
may you not work
may he not work, may she
    not work, may it not work
may we not work
may you not work
may they not work

PAST*

Affirmative
I worked
you worked
he worked
we worked
you worked
they worked

Negative
I did not work
you did not work
he did not work
we did not work
you did not work
they did not work

IMPERATIVE MOOD

Affirmative
Work

Negative
Do not work (Don't work)

Like the present subjunctive, the past may be expressed by using the auxiliary verbs "should" and "might." Otherwise, the past subjunctive has the same form as the past indicative. The subjunctive tenses not shown in this chart are the same as the indicative.

---

*The only exception to this rule is the verb "be." (See page 6)

PRINCIPAL PARTS OF IRREGULAR VERBS

Present	Past	Past Participle	Present	Past	Past Participle
bear	bore	born, borne	hide	hid	hidden
			hit	hit	hit
beat	beat	beaten	hold	held	held
become	became	become	hurt	hurt	hurt
begin	began	begun	keep	kept	kept
bend	bent	bent	know	knew	known
bet	bet	bet	lay	laid	laid
bite	bit	bitten	lead	led	led
bleed	bled	bled	leave	left	left
blow	blew	blown	lend	lent	lent
bring	brought	brought	let	let	let
build	built	built	lie [1]	lay	lain
buy	bought	bought	light	lit, lighted	lit, lighted
catch	caught	caught			
choose	chose	chosen	lose	lost	lost
come	came	come	make	made	made
cost	cost	cost	mean	meant	meant
creep	crept	crept	meet	met	met
cut	cut	cut	pay	paid	paid
deal	dealt	dealt	put	put	put
dig	dug	dug	quit	quit	quit
do	did	done	read	read	read
draw	drew	drawn	ride	rode	ridden
drink	drank	drunk	ring	rang	rung
drive	drove	driven	rise	rose	risen
eat	ate	eaten	run	ran	run
fall	fell	fallen	say	said	said
feed	fed	fed	see	saw	seen
feel	felt	felt	shake	shook	shaken
fight	fought	fought	sell	sold	sold
find	found	found	send	sent	sent
fly	flew	flown	set	set	set
forget	forgot	forgotten	shine	shone	shone
forgive	forgave	forgiven	shoot	shot	shot
freeze	froze	frozen	shrink	shrank	shrunk
get	got	got, gotten	shut	shut	shut
give	gave	given	sing	sang	sung
go	went	gone	sink	sank	sunk
grind	ground	ground	sit	sat	sat
grow	grew	grown	sleep	slept	slept
hang	hung	hung	slide	slid	slid
have	had	had	speak	spoke	spoken
hear	heard	heard	spend	spent	spent

[1] When the verb "lie" means *to tell an untruth*, it is regular: lie, lied, lied.

Present	Past	Past Participle	Present	Past	Past Participle
spread	spread	spread	tear	tore	torn
spring	sprang	sprung	tell	told	told
stand	stood	stood	think	thought	thought
steal	stole	stolen	throw	threw	thrown
stick	stuck	stuck	wake	woke, waked	waked
strike	struck	struck			
swear	swore	sworn	wear	wore	worn
sweep	swept	swept	weave	wove	woven
swim	swam	swum	win	won	won
swing	swung	swung	wind	wound	wound
take	took	taken	write	wrote	written
teach	taught	taught			

REGULAR VERBS

Present	Past	Past Participle	Present	Past	Past Participle
change	changed	changed	live	lived	lived
enjoy	enjoyed	enjoyed	stay	stayed	stayed
look	looked	looked	turn	turned	turned
like	liked	liked	wait	waited	waited
listen	listened	listened	want	wanted	wanted

All regular verbs follow this pattern, adding "ed" to form the past tense and the past participle. If the verb ends in "e," only the "d" is added.

REGULAR VERBS WITH ORTHOGRAPHIC CHANGES

Present	Past	Past Participle	Present	Past	Past Participle
carry	carried	carried	marry	married	married
cry	cried	cried	study	studied	studied
hurry	hurried	hurried	try	tried	tried

Verbs ending in "y" *preceded by a consonant* change "y" to "ı" before adding "ed."

Present	Past	Past Participle
plan	planned	planned
prefer	preferred	preferred

Regular verbs ending in a *single consonant* preceded by a *single vowel* double the final consonant before "ed" and "ing," if the verb consists of *one syllable* or if the *final syllable is stressed*. (See Lesson XXX, page 161).

APPENDIX II

90	ninety	90th	ninetieth
100	one hundred	100th	one hundredth, hundredth
101	one hundred one*	101st	one hundred first
102	one hundred two*	102d	one hundred second
150	one hundred fifty*	150th	one hundred fiftieth
1000	one thousand	1000th	one thousandth, thousandth
10,000	ten thousand	10,000th	ten thousandth
100,000	one hundred thousand	100,000th	one hundred thousandth
1,000,000	one million	1,000,000th	one millionth, millionth
1,000,000,000	one billion	1,000,000,000th	one billionth, billionth

LINEAR MEASURE

12 inches	=	1 foot
3 feet	=	1 yard
5½ yards	=	1 rod
320 rods	=	1 mile
5280 feet	=	1 mile

METRIC EQUIVALENTS

1 inch	=	2.54 centimeters
1 foot	=	30.38 centimeters
1 yard	=	.9144 meter
1 mile	=	1.6 kilometers

LIQUID MEASURE

2 pints	=	1 quart
4 quarts	=	1 gallon
1 quart	=	.9463 liter
1 gallon	=	3.7853 liters

SQUARE MEASURE

160 square rods	=	1 acre
43,560 square feet	=	1 acre
4,047 square meters	=	1 acre

ABBREVIATIONS:

inch	— in. ('')
foot, feet	— ft. (')
yard	— yd.
ounce	— oz.
pound	— lb.
pint	— pt.
quart	— qt.
gallon	— gal.

WEIGHT

16 ounces	=	1 pound
2000 pounds	=	1 ton
1 pound	=	.4536 kilogram
1 ton (U.S.)	=	907.18 kilograms
1.102 tons (U.S.)	=	1 metric ton

*In informal oral usage, these might be: *a hundred and one, a hundred and two, a hundred and fifty.* In the same way, using the indefinite article instead of "one," we often say *a thousand, a million, a billion.*

APPENDIX III

PREPARATION FOR COLLEGE ENTRANCE EXAMINATIONS

To pass the college entrance examinations, you will need a much larger vocabulary than you will get in any one textbook. To your daily studies you should add at least an hour's reading, during which you write in a notebook all the new words that you find. Write the word, look up its definition, and try to use it in conversation. Good magazines are the best source of vocabulary. Keep your notebook and go back over the words often. Try to build up a vocabulary of several thousand words—you will need it in the college entrance examinations.

A part of the College Entrance Examination will test your ability to understand spoken English. You can prepare for this by taking advantage of every opportunity to listen to records or tapes, to television programs, and to persons who are speaking English. Do not be discouraged because at first you understand very little. Try to understand just one word at a time, and persevere in listening. If you have records, play them over and over until you understand them. Another good practice is to do your studying aloud. When you read a sentence, or when you write it, repeat it aloud so that you also hear it.

The following questions will help you to understand the form of the tests:

1. You will hear: John sold his car to Henry last week.
    You will read: (A) John bought Henry's car.
    　　　　　　　(B) John is going to sell his car.
    　　　　　　　(C) Henry bought John's car.
    　　　　　　　(D) Henry is going to buy John's car.

Select from A, B, C, and D the statement that corresponds to what you heard.

264

2. You will hear: George should have studied instead of going swimming.

You will read: (A) George went swimming after he finished studying.

(B) George went swimming, but he didn't study.

(C) George didn't go swimming because he had to study.

(D) George studied after he went swimming.

3. You will hear a conversation between two people, and then a third voice will ask you a question based on the conversation.

Man: How much is this candy a pound?

Woman: The hard candy is a dollar a pound, and the chocolates are a dollar and fifty cents.

Man: I'll take half a pound of the hard candy, and two pounds of chocolates.

3d voice: How much will he have to pay for the candy he bought?

4. **Man:** Haven't you found an apartment yet?

Woman: We found a nice one, but it wasn't large enough. It had only one bedroom.

Man: How many bedrooms do you need?

Woman: Well, I have to have a room for myself, and so does my sister. Then the two boys can sleep together in the other bedroom.

3d voice: How many bedrooms do they need?

The second and third parts of the examination will test your knowledge of sentence structure, your vocabulary, and your reading comprehension. The questions will be similar to the following:

5. Change to negative form:

He wore a sport coat. _____ .

They were wearing boots. _____ .

She often wears a hat. _____ .

6. Change to interrogative form:
They want to buy some
flowers. _____ .

265

He tried to open the door. _____.

He is not going to leave. _____.

7. In the following statements, certain words are underlined. Write the question to which the underlined words are the answer:
   Example: John put <u>fifty dollars</u> in his savings account.
       Write: How much money did John put in his savings account?
         <u>Sixteen people</u> came to the meeting.

   _____?

       The meeting was <u>in the company office</u>.

   _____?

       Mr. Parker arrived <u>at half-past eight</u>.

   _____?

       $400 was collected <u>by the committee</u>.

   _____?

       They stayed <u>for two hours</u>.

   _____?

8. (A) obligation   (B) possibility   (C) probability
   Which of the above, A, B, or C, is indicated in the following sentence:
   You *must have felt tired* after the party was over.

9. Which is indicated in the following:
   John *might go* with you to the beach tomorrow.

10. Did you call Mary up last night?
    Choose the sentence that can correctly answer the question:
    (A) Yes, I did, but her line was busy.
    (B) Yes, I called up Mary in the morning.
    (C) Yes, I called up her after supper.
    (D) Yes, I forgot to call her.

11. He denied that he had been at home that night.
    Choose the sentence that most closely expresses the same idea:
    (A) He admitted that he had been at home that night.
    (B) He refused to stay at home that night.
    (C) He said that he had not been at home that night.
    (D) He argued that he had been at home that night.

12. Would you like cream with your coffee?

No, I don't _____ , thank you.
(A) like   (B) want some   (C) want any   (D) like any

13. How many stamps do you want?

I want three _____ airmail stamps, please.
(A) 15-cent   (B) 15-cents   (C) 15 cents'   (D) 15-cent's

14. The telephone seems to be out of order.

What is the matter _____ it?
(A) of   (B) for   (C) on   (D) with

15. I'd like to buy an inexpensive pen.

Will this do? It is the _____ we have.
(A) most cheap one   (B) cheapest one than
(C) cheapest one   (D) cheaper that

16. Was Frank badly injured in the accident?
Yes, the doctor says it will take him several months to _____ .
(A) get out of it   (B) get over it
(C) get it over   (D) put it off

17. Henry didn't buy a ticket for the show because he had _____ seen it.
(A) still   (B) ever   (C) already   (D) yet

18. They introduced me to some friends _____ .
(A) of their   (B) of them   (C) theirs   (D) of theirs

Vocabulary

19. An example of a *weapon* is
(A) a bracelet   (B) a screwdriver
(C) a gun   (D) a spade

20. If the two men are having a *quarrel*, they are having
(A) a discussion   (B) a disagreement
(C) an engagement   (D) a conference

21. *Disease* means most nearly
(A) fever   (B) sore throat
(C) a sharp pain   (D) sickness

22. A *wealthy* man is
(A) rich   (B) talented   (C) fortunate   (D) strong

23. I must have this belt shortened. It is too
   (A) wide　　(B) narrow　　(C) loose　　(D) tight
24. You can't fail to see the sign. It is very
   (A) confusing　　　　　　(B) conspicuous
   (C) involved　　　　　　 (D) amusing

In the following sentences, *one* of the underlined phrases is incorrect. Choose this incorrect word or phrase, and note if it is A, B, C, or D.

25. We <u>would have arrived</u> earlier if we <u>have known</u> that the lecture
   　　　　(A)　　　　　　　　　　　(B)
   <u>was scheduled</u> to begin <u>at 8:15</u> .
   　　(C)　　　　　　　 (D)

26. Mr. Mills expressed his wish that the <u>full amount</u> realized
   　　　　　　　　　　　　　　　　　(A)
   <u>from the sale</u> of the bonds <u>be turned over</u> to <u>George and I</u> .
   　　(B)　　　　　　　　　　(C)　　　　　　(D)

Reading Comprehension

You will be given a short time to read a paragraph, and then you must select from a group of four sentences the one that expresses what was said in the material that you read. All of the sentences are grammatically correct, but only one is correct in meaning.

27. *The steel industry grew up in the latter part of the nineteenth century. As railroads spread over the country, the demand for steel increased. In 1880 iron production was more than four million tons, and steel production was one million tons. The greatest of the early giants of the steel industry was Andrew Carnegie, the Scottish-born industrialist and philanthropist, who came to America in 1848, when he was a child of twelve. His parents were very poor. He worked in the telegraph and railroad businesses, where he had a successful career. In 1868 he went into the steel industry. In the next thirty-two years (the period in which American steel production came not only to equal but to surpass that of England), he built up a colossal steel empire which controlled the major part of American steel making. Then he sold his interest to a group of industrialists who formed United States Steel, and he himself spent the rest of his

---

*Adapted fom M. Smelser, *American History at a Glance* (New York: Barnes & Noble, 1961), p. 139.

life giving away his money to build libraries and to establish benevolent trust funds and research institutions.

Example: The steel industry grew up (A) in the early part of the 1800s.
(B) before 1900.
(C) after World War I.
(D) after 1900.

(The correct answer is "B".)

1. In 1880 (A) more steel was produced than iron.
(B) less iron was produced than steel.
(C) more iron was produced than steel.
(D) the production of steel was half that of iron.

2. Andrew Carnegie (A) was a native of the United States.
(B) kept control of United States Steel until his death.
(C) never worked outside the steel industry.
(D) was successful in business before going into steel making.

3. (A) American steel production never reached that of England.
(B) In 1868 England produced more steel than the United States.
(C) In 1900 the United States produced less steel than England.
(D) The United States has always surpassed England in steel production.

28. *Western civilization is the creation of the men and women who succeeded to the inheritance of the Greeks and Romans in the fifth century A.D. But no civilization is an entirely new creation; all are dependent upon the achievement of those who preceded them. Much of the Greek heritage was in turn inherited by the Romans, and the Greeks themselves were one of the most gifted peoples of the Roman Empire. Similarly, some of the Teutonic barbarians who came into possession of former Roman lands from the fourth century onward wished to maintain as much as they could of the advanced institutions of Rome, at the same time keeping their old tribal allegiances and the manners to

*Adapted from S. C. Easton, *Brief History of the Western World* (New York: Barnes & Noble, 1966), p. 1.

which they were accustomed. Nevertheless, comparatively little survived from Roman times. The Teutonic element predominated in all the western countries, and the new civilization which we call "Western" is a distinctive achievement—the work of the peoples the Romans called barbarian, grafted upon a base provided by the "classical civilization" of the Greeks and Romans.

1. (A) The Greeks inherited their civilization from the Romans.
   (B) The Greeks remained outside the Roman Empire.
   (C) The Greco-Roman civilization gave way to the beginnings of Western civilization in the fifth century.
   (D) Western civilization is a totally new and independent creation.

2. (A) Many Roman elements survived in Western civilization.
   (B) Some of the northern barbarians desired to keep Roman institutions.
   (C) The Teutonic barbarians tried to destroy all of Greco-Roman civilization.
   (D) Nothing of classical civilization survived the barbarian invasions.

ANSWERS TO QUESTIONS

1. C
2. B
3. $3.50
4. three bedrooms
5. He didn't wear a sport coat.
   They were not wearing boots.
   She does not often wear a hat.
6. Do they want to buy some (or any) flowers?
   Did he try to open the door?
   Isn't he going to leave?
7. How many people came to the meeting?
   Where was the meeting?
   When did Mr. Parker arrive?
   How much money was collected by the committee?
   How long did they stay?
8. C
9. B
10. A
11. C
12. C
13. A

14. D
15. C
16. B
17. C
18. D
19. C
20. B
21. D
22. A
23. C
24. B
25. B
26. D
27. 1—C
    2—D
    3—B
28. 1—C
    2—B

VOCABULARY[1]

A

a, an	ə,ən
able	'ebḷ
about	ə'baʊt
accept	ək'sɛpt
accident	'æksədənt
accidentally	ˌæksə'dɛntḷɪ
account	ə'kaʊnt
accountant	ə'kaʊntənt
accustomed	ə'kʌstəmd
across	ə'krɔs
active	'æktɪv
actress	'æktrɪs
Adams	'ædəmz
address	ə'drɛs
advance	əd'væns
advice	əd'vaɪs
advise	əd'vaɪz
advised	əd'vaɪzd
afraid	ə'fred
after	'æftɚ
afternoon	ˌæftɚ'nun
age	edʒ
agency	'edʒənsɪ
agent	'edʒənt
ago	ə'go
agree	ə'gri

ahead	ə'hɛd
air	ɛr
airport	'ɛrport
alarm	ə'lɑrm
Alaska	ə'læskə
Albert	'ælbɚt
Alice	'ælɪs
alike	ə'laɪk
all	ɔl
allow	ə'laʊ
all right	ˌɔl'raɪt
almost	ɔl'most
alone	ə'lon
along	ə'lɔŋ
also	'ɔlso
always	'ɔlwɪz,'ɔlwez
am	æm
ambulance	'æmbjələns
among	ə'mʌŋ
amount	ə'maʊnt
and	ænd,ənd
Anderson	'ændɚsṇ
Andes	'ændiz
angry	'æŋgrɪ
animal	'ænəmḷ
another	ə'nʌðɚ
answer	'ænsɚ
any	'ɛnɪ

---

[1] Phonetic pronunciations used by permission. From *A Pronouncing Dictionary of American English* © 1953 by G. & C. Merriam Co., Publishers of the Merriam-Webster Dictionaries.

anybody 'ɛnɪ,bɑdɪ
anyone 'ɛnɪ,wʌn
anything 'ɛnɪ,θɪŋ
anywhere 'ɛnɪ,hwɛr
apartment ə'pɑrtmənt
appetite 'æpə,taɪt
apple 'æpl̩
application æplə'keʃən
appointment ə'pɔɪntmənt
April 'eprəl
are ɑr
aren't ɑrnt
Argentina ɑrdʒən'tinə
army 'ɑrmɪ
around ə'raʊnd
arrive ə'raɪv
arrived ə'raɪvd
art ɑrt
article 'ɑrtɪkl
artist 'ɑrtɪst
as æz,əz
ask æsk
asked æskt
asleep ə'slip
aspirin 'æspərɪn
assistant ə'sɪstənt
assume ə'sjum, ə'sum
at æt
ate et
Atlantic ət'læntɪk
attack ə'tæk
attend ə'tɛnd
August 'ɔgəst
aunt ænt
automatic ,ɔtə'mætɪk
automobile ,ɔtə'mobil
avenue 'ævə,nu
avoid ə'vɔɪd
aware ə'wɛr
away ə'we

B

baby 'bebɪ
  babies 'bebɪz
back bæk
bad bæd
badly 'bædlɪ
Baker 'bekɚ
ballet ,bæ'le
bank bæŋk
Barbara bɑrbərə
bath bæθ
bathroom 'bæθrum
bay be
be bi
beach bitʃ
beauty 'bjutɪ
  beautiful 'bjutəfəl
because bɪ'kɔz
become bɪ'kʌm
  became bɪ'kem
bed bɛd
bedroom 'bɛd,rum
been bɪn
begin bɪ'gɪn
  began bɪ'gæn
  begun bɪ'gʌn
behind bɪ'haɪnd
believe bə'liv
believed bə'livd
belong bə'lɔŋ
belonged bə'lɔŋd
belt bɛlt
Bermuda bɚ'mjudə
best bɛst
better 'bɛtɚ
Betty 'bɛtɪ
between bə'twin
bicycle 'baɪ,sɪkl̩
big bɪg
bigger 'bɪgɚ

biggest 'bɪgɪst
bill bɪl
Biltmore 'bɪltmor
biology baɪ'alədʒɪ
birthday bɝθde
black blæk
block blɑk
blond blɑnd
blow blo
    blew blu
    blown blon
blue blu, blɪu
board bord
boat bot
Bob bɑb
book bʊk
bookstore 'bʊkstor
bore bor
borrow 'boro
Boston 'bostn̩
both boθ
bother 'bɑðɚ
bought bot
box bɑks
boxes 'bɑksɪz
boy bɔɪ
boys bɔɪz
bread brɛd
breakfast 'brɛkfəst
Brent brɛnt
bright braɪt
bring brɪŋ
bringing brɪŋɪŋ
Broadway 'brɔdwe
brother 'brʌðɚ
brought brɔt
brown braʊn
brunet brunɛt
brush brʌʃ
build bɪld
building 'bɪldɪŋ

built bɪlt
burn bɝn
burned bɝnd
bus bʌs
business 'bɪznɪs
busy 'bɪzɪ
buy baɪ
by baɪ

C

cafeteria ,kæfə'tɪrɪə
cake kek
call kɔl
called kɔld
came kem
camera 'kæmərə
can kæn
Canada 'kænədə
cancel 'kænsl̩
candy 'kændɪ
captain 'kæptɪn
car kɑr
care kɛr
careful 'kɛrfəl
carefully 'kɛrfəlɪ
Caribbean ,kærə'biən,
    kə'rɪbɪən
Carol 'kærəl
carry 'kærɪ
Carter 'kɑrtɚ
cash kæʃ
catch kætʃ
    caught kɔt
catercorner 'kætɚ,kɔrnɚ
cent sɛnt
center 'sɛntɚ
centered 'sɛntɚd
central 'sɛntrəl
chain tʃen
chair tʃɛr

chairman   tʃɛrmən
chamber   'tʃembɚ
change   'tʃendʒ
changed   tʃendʒd
changes   'tʃendʒɪz
Chapman   'tʃæpmən
charge   tʃɑrdʒ
Charles   tʃɑrlz
cheap   tʃip
cheaper   tʃipɚ
check   tʃɛk
cheeks   tʃiks
chemistry   'kɛmɪstrɪ
Chesapeake   'tʃɛsə,pik
Chicago   ʃɪ'kɔgo
child   tʃaɪld
children   'tʃɪldrɪn
choose   tʃuz
   chose   tʃoz
   chosen   'tʃozn̩
Christmas   'krɪsməs
church   tʃɚtʃ
cigarette   sɪgə'rɛt
city   'sɪtɪ
class   klæs
classroom   'klæs,rum
clean   klin
cleaned   klind
cleaner   klinɚ
clerk   klɝk
clever   klɛvɚ
clock   klɑk
clothes (noun)   kloz
clothing   'kloðɪŋ
cloud   klaʊd
cloudy   'klaʊdɪ
club   klʌb
coast   kost
coat   kot
coffee   'kɔfɪ
coffeepot   'kɔfɪ,pɑt

cold   kold
college   'kɑlɪdʒ
colony   'kɑlənɪ
color   'kʌlɚ
come   kʌm
   came   kem
commerce   'kɑmɚs
commercial   kə'mɝʃəl
committee   kə'mɪtɪ
company   'kʌmpənɪ
compel   kəm'pɛl
concern   kən'sɝn
concerned   kən'sɝnd
concert   'kɑnsɚt
condition   kən'dɪʃən
consider   kən'sɪdɚ
continue   kən'tɪnju
contract   'kɑntrækt
control   kən'trol
controlled   kən'trold
cook   kʊk
cookies   'kʊkɪz
cool   kul
corner   'kɔrnɚ
correspondence
      ,kɔrə'spandəns
cost   kɔst
cough   kɔf
coughed   kɔft
could   kʊd
country   'kʌntrɪ
course   kors
cousin   'kʌzn̩
cowboy   'kaʊbɔɪ
crime   kraɪm
cross   krɔs
crossed   krɔst
crosses   'krɔsɪz
crowd   kraʊd
crowded   'kraʊdɪd
cry   kraɪ

cried   kraɪd
crying   kraɪ-ɪŋ
Cuba   kjubə
Cuban   kjubən
cup   kʌp
cut   kʌt

D

damage   ˈdæmɪdʒ
damaged   ˈdæmɪdʒd
damages   ˈdæmɪdʒɪs
dance   dæns
dangerous   ˈdendʒərəs
dark   dɑrk
date   det
Davis   ˈdevɪs
deal   dil
death   dɛθ
December   dɪˈsɛmbər
decide   dɪˈsaɪd
decided   dɪˈsaɪdɪd
deep   dip
deeper   ˈdipər
deepest   ˈdipɪst
dentist   ˈdɛntɪst
Denver   ˈdɛnvər
department   dɪˈpɑrtmənt
desk   dɛsk
Dick   dɪk
Dickens   ˈdɪkɪnz
dictionary   ˈdɪkʃən,ɛrɪ
did   dɪd
didn't   ˈdɪdn̩t
die   daɪ
died   daɪd
dies   daɪz
differ   ˈdɪfər
different   ˈdɪfənt
difficult   ˈdɪfə,kʌlt
dinner   ˈdɪnər

276

directory   dəˈrɛktərɪ
discuss   dɪsˈkʌs
discussed   dɪsˈkʌst
discusses   dɪsˈkʌsɪz
dish   dɪʃ
dishes   ˈdɪʃɪz
Dixon   ˈdɪksn̩
does   dʌz
doesn't   ˈdʌzn̩t
dog   dɔg
dollar   ˈdɑlər
Don   dɑn
done   dʌn
don't   dont
door   dor
doorbell   ˈdorbɛl
dormitory   ˈdɔrmə,torɪ
double   ˈdʌbl̩
down   daʊn
downtown   ˈdaʊnˈtaʊn
drawer   ˈdrɔər
dress   drɛs
dressed   drɛst
dresses   ˈdrɛsɪz
dressmaker   ˈdrɛs,mekər
drink   drɪŋk
    drank   dræŋk
drive   draɪv
    drove   drov
    driven   ˈdrɪvən
drop   drɑp
dropped   drɑpt
drugstore   ˈdrʌg,stor
dry   draɪ
during   dʊrɪŋ

E

early   ˈɝlɪ
earlier   ˈɝlɪər
earn   ɝn

earned ɝnd
east ist
eastern 'istən
easy 'izɪ
easier 'izɪɚ
easily 'izɪlɪ
eat it
    ate et
    eaten 'itn̩
Edward 'ɛdwɚd
eight et
eighteenth e'tinθ
Eileen aɪ'lin
elect ɪ'lɛkt
elected ɪ'lɛktɪd
electric ɪ'lɛktrɪk
eleven ɪ'lɛvən
Ellis 'ɛlɪs
else ɛls
empire 'ɛmpaɪr
employ ɪm'plɔɪ
end ɛnd
ended 'ɛndɪd
endorse ɪn'dɔrs
engage ɪn'gedʒ
engaged ɪn'gedʒd
engineer ,ɛndʒə'nɪr
English 'ɪŋglɪʃ
enjoy ɪn'dʒɔɪ
enjoyed ɪn'dʒɔɪd
enlarge ɪn'lardʒ
enough ə'nʌf
enter 'ɛntɚ
entered 'ɛntɚd
envelope (noun) 'ɛnʌə,lop
eraser ɪ'resɚ
Europe 'jʊrəp
Evans 'ɛvənz
Evelyn 'ɛvəlɪn
even 'ivən
evening 'ivnɪŋ

ever 'ɛvɚ
Everest 'ɛvərɪst
every 'ɛvrɪ
everybody 'ɛvrɪ,badɪ
everyone 'ɛvrɪ,wʌn
everything 'ɛvrɪ,θɪŋ
everywhere 'ɛvrɪ,hwɛr
exact ɪg'zækt
examination ɪgzæmɪ'neʃən
excel ɪk'sɛl
excellent 'ɛkslənt
execute 'ɛksɪ,kjut
exercise 'ɛksɚ,saɪz
exhaust ɪg'zɔst
exhausted ɪg'zɔstɪd
expect ɪk'spɛkt
expected ɪk'spɛktɪd
expense ɪk'spɛns
expenses ɪk'spɛnsɪz
expensive ɪk'spɛnsɪv
explain ɪk'splen
explosion ɪk'sploʒən
express ɪk'sprɛs
extra 'ɛkstrə
eye aɪ
eyes aɪz

F

fact fækt
factory 'fæktərɪ
fail fel
failed feld
failure 'feljɚ
fall fɔl
    fell fɛl
family 'fæməlɪ
families 'fæməlɪz
fan fæn
fantastic fæn'tæstɪk
far far

farmer   'farmɚ
farther   'farðɚ
fast   fæst
faster   'fæstɚ
fat   fæt
    fatter   'fætɚ
father   'faðɚ
favorite   'fevərɪt
February   'fɛbju,ɛrɪ
federal   'fɛdərəl
feel   fil
    felt   fɛlt
feed   fid
    fed   fɛd
feet   fit
few   fju
fewer   'fjuɚ
fewest   'fjuɪst
fifteen   fɪf'tin
fifth   fɪfθ
fifty   'fɪftɪ
fill   fɪl
filled   fɪld
Finch   fɪntʃ
find   faɪnd
    found   faund
fine   faɪn
finish   'fɪnɪʃ
finished   'fɪnɪʃt
finishes   'fɪnɪʃɪz
first   fɝst
Fisher   'fɪʃɚ
five   faɪv
fix   fɪks
fixed   fɪkst
fixes   'fɪksɪz
flight   flaɪt
floor   flor
Florence   'flɔrəns
Florida   'flɔrədə
flower   'flauɚ

fly   flaɪ
    flew   flu
    flown   flon
follow   'falo
followed   'falod
fool   ful
foot   fut
    feet   fit
for   fɔr
Forbes   fɔrbz
force   fɔrs
forced   fɔrst
forces   'fɔrsɪz
forget   fɚ'gɛt
    forgot   fɚ'gat
    forgotten   fɚ'gatn̩
form   fɔrm
formed   fɔrmd
forty   'fɔrtɪ
forward   'fɔrwɚd
Foster   'fɔstɚ
four   fɔr
fourteen   fɔr'tin
Frank   fræŋk
Franklin   'fræŋklɪn
French   frɛntʃ
frequently   'frikwəntlɪ
Friday   'fraɪdɪ
friend   frɛnd
from   fram
front   frʌnt
fulfill   ful'fɪl
furniture   'fɝnɪtʃɚ

G

gallon   'gælən
game   gem
garage   gə'raʒ
garden   'gardn̩
garment   'garmənt

278

gasoline	'gæsḷ,in	half	hæf
gates	gets	hall	hɔl
generous	'dʒɛnərəs	hand	hænd
gentleman	'dʒɛntḷmən	happy	'hæpɪ
George	dʒɔrdʒ	happier	'hæpɪɚ
German	'dʒɝmən	hard	hɑrd
Germany	'dʒɝmənɪ	harder	'hɑrdɚ
get	gɛt	Harold	'hærəld
got	gɑt	Harris	'hærəs
gotten	'gɑtṇ	Harrison	'hærəsṇ
Gibbs	gɪbz	has	hæz
girl	gɝl	hasn't	'hæzn̩t
give	gɪv	hat	hæt
gave	gev	have	hæv
given	'gɪvən	haven't	'hævṇt
glad	glæd	Hawaii	hə'wɑ-i
glasses	'glæsɪz	he	hi
gloves	glʌvz	headache	'hɛd,ɛk
go	go	health	hɛlθ
goes	goz	hear	hɪr
going	'go-ɪŋ	heard	hɝd
gone	gɔn	heart	hɑrt
good	gʊd	heater	'hitɚ
goodbye	gʊd'baɪ	Helen	'hɛlɪn
Grace	gres	he'll	hil
graduate (verb)	'grædʒʊ,et	help	hɛlp
grandfather	'græn,fɑðɚ	helped	hɛlpt
grandmother	'græn,mʌðɚ	Henry	'hɛnrɪ
grasp	græsp	her	hɝ
great	gret	Herbert	'hɝbɚt
Greece	gris	here	hɪr
green	grin	hers	hɝz
grocery	'grosɚɪ	herself	hɚ'sɛlf
guest	gɛst	he's	hiz
gulf	gʌlf	hide	haɪd
gun	gʌn	hid	hɪd
		hidden	'hɪdn̩
		high	haɪ

H

		higher	'haɪɚ
habit	'hæbɪt	hill	hɪl
had	hæd	Hilton	'hɪltən

him hɪm
himself hɪm'sɛlf
his hɪz
hobby 'habɪ
hold hold
   held hɛld
Holmes homz
home hom
honest 'anɪst
honestly 'anɪstlɪ
hope hop
hospital 'haspɪtl̩
hot hat
hotter 'hatɚ
hotel ho'tɛl
hour aʊr
house (noun) haʊs
houses (noun) 'haʊzɪz
housewife 'haʊs,waɪf
housework 'haʊs,wɝk
how haʊ
huge hjudʒ
Hugo 'hjugo
hundred 'hʌndrəd
hungry 'hʌŋgrɪ
Hunter 'hʌntɚ
hurry 'hɝɪ
hurried 'hɝɪd
husband 'hʌzbənd

I

I aɪ
icebox 'aɪs,baks
I'd aɪd
idea aɪ'diə
if ɪf
I'll aɪl
illegal ɪ'ligl̩
I'm aɪm
immigration ɪmə'greʃən

important ɪm'pɔrtnt
inch ɪntʃ
inches 'ɪntʃɪz
income 'ɪn,kʌm
Indian 'ɪndɪən
inefficient ,ɪnə'fɪʃənt
influence 'ɪnfluəns
influenza ɪnflʊ'ɛnzə
inform ɪn'fɔrm
informed ɪn'fɔrmd
injure 'ɪndʒɚ
injured 'ɪndʒɚd
insist ɪn'sɪst
insisted ɪn'sɪstɪd
instead ɪn'stɛd
intend ɪn'tɛnd
intended ɪn'tɛndɪd
interest 'ɪntərɪst
interested 'ɪntə,rɛstɪd
interesting 'ɪntə,rɛstɪŋ
international ,ɪntɚ'næʃənl̩
introduce ,ɪntrə'djus
invent ɪn'vɛnt
invention ɪn'vɛnʃən
invite ɪn'vaɪt
invited ɪn'vaɪtɪd
invitation ,ɪnvə'teʃən
iron 'aɪɚn
is ɪz
isn't 'ɪzn̩t
it ɪt
it'll 'ɪtl̩
its ɪts
itself ɪt'sɛlf
I've aɪv

J

Jackson 'dʒæksn̩
James dʒemz
Jane dʒen

January   'dʒænjʊ,ɛrɪ
Jefferson 'dʒɛfɚsn̩
Jennie   'dʒɛnɪ
Jerry   'dʒɛrɪ
jet   dʒɛt
Jim   dʒɪm
job   dʒab
John   dʒan
Johnson   'dʒansn̩
judge   dʒʌdʒ
judges   'dʒʌdʒɪz
July   dʒu'laɪ
June   dʒun
just   dʒʌst
justice   'dʒʌstɪs

K

Karen   'kærən
Kennedy   'kɛnədɪ
keep   kip
kept   kɛpt
key   ki
kid   kɪd
kill   kɪl
killed   kɪld
king   kɪŋ
Kingston   'kɪŋz-tən
kitchen   'kɪtʃən
knife   naɪf
knives   naɪvz
know   no
    knew   nju
    known non

L

lack   læk
lady   'ledɪ
    ladies 'ledɪz

lake   lek
lakeshore 'lekʃor
lane   len
language   'læŋgwɪdʒ
languages 'læŋgwɪdʒɪz
large   lɑrdʒ
larger   'lɑrdʒɚ
largest   'lɑrdʒɪst
last   læst
late   let
lately   'letlɪ
later   'letɚ
laugh   læf
laughed   læft
laughing   'læfɪŋ
law   lɔ
laws   lɔz
lawyer   'lɔjɚ
lazy   'lezɪ
lead   lid
leader   'lidɚ
led   lɛd
leaf   lif
leaves   livz
leak   lik
learn   lɝn
learned   lɝnd
leave   liv
    left   lɛft
least   list
lecture   'lektʃɚ
lend   lɛnd
    lent   lɛnt
less   lɛs
lesson   lɛsn̩
let   lɛt
lets   lɛts
letter   'lɛtɚ
Lexington 'lɛksɪŋtən
library   'laɪ,brɛrɪ
lie   laɪ

281

lied	laɪd		
lies	laɪz		
light	laɪt		**M**
like	laɪk	machine	mə'ʃin
liked	laɪkt	Macy	'mesɪ
life	laɪf	Madison	'mædəsn̩
lives (noun)	laɪvz	magazine	'mægə,zin
Linda	'lɪndə	maid	med
Lisa	'lisə	main	men
Lisbon	'lɪzbən	make	mek
list	lɪst	made	med
listen	'lɪsn̩	man	mæn
listened	'lɪsn̩d	men	mɛn
literary	'lɪtə,rɛrɪ	manager	'mænɪdʒɚ
little	'lɪtl̩	many	'mɛnɪ
live (verb)	lɪv	March	mɑrtʃ
lived	lɪvd	Margaret	'mɑrgərɪt
lives	lɪvz	marry	'mærɪ
local	'lokl̩	married	'mærɪd
London	'lʌndən	Mary	'mɛrɪ, 'merɪ
long	lɔŋ	match	mætʃ
longer	'lɔŋgɚ	matched	mætʃt
longest	'lɔŋgɪst	matches	'mætʃɪz
look	lʊk	matter	'mætɚ
looked	lʊkt	may	me
lookout	'lʊk,aʊt	might	maɪt
lose	luz	maybe	'mebɪ
lost	lɔst	mayor	'meɚ
lot	lɑt	me	mi
lots	lɑts	meal	mil
loud	laʊd	meat market	'mit'mɑrkɪt
Louis	'luɪs	mechanic	mə'kænɪk
Louise	lu'iz	medical	'mɛdɪkl̩
love	lʌv	medicine	'mɛdəsn̩
loved	lʌvd	meet	mit
loves	lʌvz	met	mɛt
low	lo	merchant	'mɝtʃənt
lower	'loɚ	Miami	maɪ'æmɪ
luck	lʌk	midnight	'mɪd,naɪt
lucky	'lʌkɪ	mile	maɪl
lunch	lʌntʃ	milk	mɪlk
		Miller	'mɪlɚ

millimeter   'mɪlə,mitɚ
mind   maɪnd
mine   maɪn
minute   'mɪnɪt
mirror   'mɪrɚ
Miss   mɪs
mistake   məs'tek
Mitchell   'mɪtʃəl
Monday   'mʌndɪ
money   'mʌnɪ
month   mʌnθ
more   mor
morning   'mɔrnɪŋ
Morris   'mɔrɪs
Morton   'mɔrtn̩
most   most
mother   mʌðɚ
motor   motɚ
mount   maʊnt
mountain   'maʊntn̩
mouse   maʊs
   mice   maɪs
move   muv
moved   muvd
movie   muvɪ
Mr.   'mɪstɚ
Mrs.   'mɪsɪz
much   mʌtʃ
music   'mjuzɪk
must   mʌst
my   maɪ
myself   maɪ'sɛlf

N

name   nem
nap   næp
narrow   'næro
narrower   'nærəwɚ
Nashville   'næʃ,vɪl

national   'næʃənl̩
near   nɪr
nearby   nɪr'baɪ
need   nid
negligence   'nɛglədʒəns
neighbor   'nebɚ
neither   'niðɚ
nervous   'nɝvəs
never   'nɛvɚ
new   nju
newer   'njuɚ
newest   'njuɪst
news   njuz
newspaper   'njuzpepɚ
New Orleans   nju'ɔrlɪənz
New York   nju'jɔrk
next   nɛkst
nice   naɪs
nicer   'naɪsɚ
nicest   'naɪsɪst
night   naɪt
nine   naɪn
nineteen   naɪn'tin
ninety   'naɪntɪ
no   no
nobody   'no,badɪ
noise   nɔɪz
noisy   'nɔɪzɪ
nominate   'namə,net
noon   nun
north   nɔrθ
northern   'nɔrðɚn
Norton   'nɔrtn̩
not   nat
notebook   'not,bʊk
nothing   'nʌθɪŋ
notice   'notɪs
novel   'navl̩
November   no'vɛmbɚ
now   naʊ
nowhere   'no,hwɛr

number   'nʌmbɚ
nurse   nɝs

O

obey   ə'be
obeyed   ə'bed
object (verb)   əb'dʒɛkt
occur   ə'kɝ
occurred   ə'kɝd
occurrence   ə'kɝəns
ocean   'oʃən
o'clock   ə'klɑk
October   ɑk'tobɚ
of   ɑv, ʌv
off   ɔf
office   'ɔfɪs
officer   'ɔfəsɚ
offices   'ɔfəsɪz
often   'ɔfən
Ohio   o'haɪo
old   old
older   'oldɚ
oldest   'oldɪst
Olga   'ɑlgə
on   ɑn
once   wʌns
one   wʌn
oneself   wʌn'sɛlf
only   'onlɪ
open   'opən
opened   'opənd
order   'ɔrdɚ
other   'ʌðɚ
ought   ɔt
our   aʊr
ours   aʊrz
ourselves   aʊr'sɛlvz
out   aʊt
over   'ovɚ
oversleep,   ,ovɚ'slip

overslept   ,ovɚ'slɛpt
own   on
owned   ond
owner   'onɚ

P

Pacific   pə'sɪfɪk
package   'pækɪdʒ
paint   pent
painted   'pentɪd
paintings   'pentɪŋz
pair   pɛr
palm   pɑm
paper   'pepɚ
parents   'pɛrənts
Paris   'pærɪs
park   pɑrk
parked   pɑrkt
Parker   'pɑrkɚ
party   'pɑrtɪ
patient   'peʃənt
Paul   pɔl·
pay   pe
    paid   ped
paying   'pe-ɪŋ
pencil   'pɛnsl̩
penny   'pɛnɪ
people   'pipl̩
perhaps   pɚ'hæps
permit   pɚ'mɪt
permitted   pɚ'mɪtɪd
person   'pɝsn̩
Peterson   'pitɚsn̩
petition   pə'tɪʃən
Philip   'fɪləp
philosopher   fə'lɑsəfɚ
phone   fon
physical   'fɪzɪkl̩
pick   pɪk
picked   pɪkt

picture 'pɪktʃɚ
pie paɪ
pipe paɪp
plan plæn
planned plænd
plane plen
plastic 'plæstɪk
play ple
played pled
playing ple-ɪŋ
please pliz
pleasant 'plɛzn̩t
pleasure 'plɛʒɚ
plenty 'plɛntɪ
plumber 'plʌmɚ
pocketbook 'pakɪt,bʊk
poem 'po-ɪm
poetry 'po-ɪtrɪ
point pɔɪnt
pole pol
police pə'lis
policeman pə'lismən
possible 'pasəbl̩
post card 'post'kard
post office 'post,ɔfɪs
Powers 'paʊɚz
prefer prɪ'fɚ
preferred prɪ'fɚd
prepare prɪ'pɛr
present (noun) 'prɛzn̩t
presents (noun) 'prɛzn̩ts
present (verb) prɪ'zɛnt
presented (verb)
    prɪ'zɛntɪd
presents (verb) prɪ'zɛnts
president 'prɛzədənt
pretty 'prɪtɪ, pɚtɪ
previous 'privɪəs
price praɪs
prison 'prɪzn̩
prize praɪz

probably 'prabəblɪ
professor prə'fɛsɚ
program 'progræm
promote prə'mot
proposal prə'pozl̩
propose prə'poz
public 'pʌblɪk
purpose 'pɝpəs
purse pɝs
put pʊt

Q

quarter 'kwɔrtɚ
question 'kwɛstʃən
quick kwɪk
quickly kwɪklɪ
quiet 'kwaɪət
quietly 'kwaɪətlɪ
quite kwaɪt

R

radio 'redɪ,o
railing 'relɪŋ
railroad 'rel,rod
rain ren
rained rend
rainy 'renɪ
Ralph rælf
rapid 'ræpɪd
rather 'ræðɚ
razor 'rezɚ
reach ritʃ
reached ritʃt
read rid
    read rɛd
ready 'rɛdɪ
really 'rɪəlɪ
receive rɪ'siv

recommend rɛkə'mɛnd
record (noun) 'rɛkəd
red rɛd
refer rɪ'fɝ
referred rɪ'fɝd
reference 'rɛfərəns
refreshments rɪ'frɛʃmənts
refrigerator
    rɪ'frɪdʒə,retɚ
relative 'rɛlətɪv
remain rɪ'men
rent rɛnt
rented 'rɛntɪd
repair rɪ'pɛr
repeat rɪ'pit
report rɪ'port
require rɪ'kwaɪr
reservation ,rɛzɚ've ʃən
resign rɪ'zaɪn
rest rɛst
restaurant 'rɛstərənt
reward rɪ'wɔrd
rich rɪtʃ
Richard 'rɪtʃɚd
rid rɪd
ride raɪd
    rode rod
right raɪt
ring rɪŋ
    rang ræŋ
    rung rʌŋ
river 'rɪvɚ
rob rɑb
Robert 'rɑbɚt
rocky 'rɑkɪ
Rogers 'rɑdʒɚz
Ronald 'rɑnl̩d
roof ruf
room rum
rooms rumz

run rʌn
    ran ræn
Russell 'rʌsl̩
Ruth ruθ

S

safe sef
safely 'seflɪ
said sɛd
Saint Louis 'sent'luɪs
salary 'sælərɪ
sale sel
salesman 'selzmən
same sem
sandwich 'sændwɪtʃ
Saturday 'sætɚdɪ
save sev
saved sevd
say se
    said sɛd
    says sɛz
scene sin
school skul
Scott skɑt
seasick 'sisɪk
seat sit
secondhand 'sɛkənd'hænd
secret 'sikrɪt
secretary 'sɛkrə,tɛrɪ
see si
    saw sɔ
    seen sin
seeing si-ɪŋ
self sɛlf
selfish 'sɛlfɪʃ
sell sɛl
    sold sold
send sɛnd
    sent sɛnt

sentence	'sɛntəns	sign	saɪn
September	sɛp'tɛmbɚ	signed	saɪnd
servant	'sɝvənt	silly	'sɪlɪ
set	sɛt	simple	'sɪmpl̩
seven	'sɛvən	simpler	'sɪmplɚ
seventeen	ˌsɛvən'tin	since	sɪns
seventy	'sɛvəntɪ	sing	sɪŋ
several	'sɛvərəl	sang	sæŋ
sew	so	sung	sʌŋ
sewed	sod	sister	'sɪstɚ
sewing	so-ɪŋ	sit	sɪt
shallow	ʃælo	sat	sæt
shame	ʃem	sitter	'sɪtɚ
sharp	ʃɑrp	six	sɪks
shave	ʃev	sixteen	sɪks'tin
she	ʃi	sixth	sɪksθ
sheep	ʃip	sixty	'sɪkstɪ
she'd	ʃid	sky	skaɪ
she'll	ʃil	sleep	slip
she's	ʃiz	slept	slɛpt
shine	ʃaɪn	sleepy	'slipɪ
shone	ʃon	slender	'slɛndɚ
ship	ʃɪp	slow	slo
shipped	ʃɪpt	slower	'sloɚ
shirt	ʃɝt	small	smɔl
shoe	ʃu	smaller	'smɔlɚ
shoes	ʃuz	smell	smɛl
shop	ʃɑp	smoke	smok
short	ʃɔrt	smoked	smokt
shorter	'ʃɔrtɚ	smoking	'smokɪŋ
shortest	'ʃɔrtɪst	so	so
shorten	'ʃɔrtn̩	soap	sop
should	ʃʊd	socks	sɑks
shouldn't	'ʃʊdn̩t	soft	sɔft
shout	ʃaʊt	sold	sold
show	ʃo	soldier	'soldʒɚ
shower	'ʃaʊɚ	some	sʌm
sick	sɪk	somebody	'sʌmˌbɑdɪ
sickness	'sɪknɪs	someone	'sʌmˌwʌn
side	saɪd	something	'sʌmˌθɪŋ

sometimes	'sʌm,taɪmz
somewhere	'sʌm,hwɛr
son	sʌn
song	sɔŋ
soon	sun
sooner	'sunɚ
sorry	'sɔrɪ
sound	saʊnd
south	saʊθ
southern	'sʌðɚn
spare	spɛr
speak	spik
spoke	spok
spoken	'spokən
speaker	'spikɚ
spend	spɛnd
spent	spɛnt
spring	sprɪŋ
stammer	'stæmɚ
stamp	stæmp
stand	stænd
stood	stʊd
Stanton	'stæntən
start	stɑrt
started	'stɑrtɪd
state	stet
statesman	'stetsmən
station	'steʃən
stationery	'steʃən,ɛrɪ
Statler	'stætlɚ
stay	ste
stayed	sted
steal	stil
stole	stol
stolen	'stolən
steering	'stɪrɪŋ
stenographer	stə'nɑgrəfɚ
still	stɪl
stockings	'stɑkɪŋz
stop	stɑp
stopped	stɑpt

store	stor
storekeeper	'stor,kipɚ
storm	stɔrm
story	'storɪ
street	strit
stripe	straɪp
striped	straɪpt
student	'stjudn̩t
study	'stʌdɪ
studied	'stʌdɪd
studying	'stʌdɪ-ɪŋ
stun	stʌn
subway	'sʌb,we
succeed	sək'sid
success	sək'sɛs
sudden	sʌdn̩
sugar	'ʃʊgɚ
suggest	səg'dʒɛst
suggested	səg'dʒɛstɪd
suit	sjut, sut
suitcase	'sut,kes
summer	'sʌmɚ
sun	sʌn
Sunday	'sʌndɪ
superior	sə'pɪrɪɚ
supermarket	'supɚ,mɑrkɪt
supper	'sʌpɚ
supply	səp'laɪ
suppose	sə'poz
supposed	sə'pozd
surprise	sə'praɪz
sure	ʃʊr
sweater	'swɛtɚ
sweet	swit
sweetly	'switlɪ
swim	swɪm
swimming	'swɪmɪŋ

T

table	'tebl̩
tailor	'telɚ

take   tek
    took   tʊk
    taken   'tekən
talk   tɔk
talked   tɔkt
tall   tɔl
taller   'tɔlɚ
tallest   'tɔlɪst
tank   tæŋk
tardy   'tɑrdɪ
tardiness   'tɑrdɪnɪs
taste   test
taught   tɔt
tax   tæks
taxi   'tæksɪ
Taylor   'telɚ
tea   ti
teach   titʃ
teacher   'titʃɚ
team   tim
tear (verb)   tɛr
teen-age   'tin,edʒ
telegram   'tɛlə,græm
telephone   'tɛlə,fon
television   'tɛlə,vɪʒən
tell   tɛl
    told   told
tennis   'tɛnɪs
tenth   tɛnθ
terrible   'tɛrəbl
Texas   'tɛksəs
than   ðæn
thank   θæŋk
that   ðæt
the   ðə, ðɪ
theater   'θiətɚ
their   ðɛr
Thelma   'θɛlmə
them   ðɛm
themselves   ðɛm'sɛlvz
then   ðɛn

there   ðɛr
these   ðiz
they   ðe
they'll   ðel
they're   ðɛr, ðer
they've   ðev
thick   θɪk
thief   θif
thieves   θivz
thin   θɪn
thing   θɪŋ
think   θɪŋk
third   θɝd
thirsty   'θɝstɪ
thirteen   θɝ'tin
thirty   'θɝtɪ
this   ðɪs
Thomas   'tɑməs
Thompson   'tɑmpsn̩
those   ðoz
though   ðo
thought   θɔt
thousand   'θaʊznd̩
three   θri
through   θru
throw   θro
    threw   θru
    thrown   θron
thunder   'θʌndɚ
Thursday   'θɝzdɪ
ticket   'tɪkɪt
time   taɪm
timid   'tɪmɪd
tired   taɪrd
title   'taɪtl̩
to   tu
today   tə'de
together   tə'gɛðɚ
Tom   tɑm
tomorrow   tə'mɔro
tonight   tə'naɪt

too   tu
took   tʊk
tooth   tuθ
    teeth   tiθ
toothpaste   'tuθ,pest
touch   tʌtʃ
town   taʊn
track   træk
trade   tred
trading   'tredɪŋ
traffic   'træfɪk
train   tren
travel   'trævl̩
treasurer   'trɛʒərɚ
tree   tri
trip   trɪp
trouble   'trʌbl̩
trousers   'traʊzɚz
true   tru
truth   truθ
try   traɪ
trying   'traɪ-ɪŋ
Tuesday   'tjuzdɪ
Tulsa   'tʌlsə
turn   tɝn
turned   tɝnd
twelve   twɛlv
twenty   'twɛntɪ
two   tu
Tyler   'taɪlɚ
type   taɪp
typewriter   'taɪp,raɪtɚ
typing   'taɪpɪŋ
typist   'taɪpɪst

U

uncle   'ʌŋkl̩
understand   ,ʌndɚ'stænd
    understood
      ,ʌndɚ'stʊd

United States
      ju'naɪtɪd'stets
university   ,junə'vɝsətɪ
unless   ən'lɛs
until   ən'tɪl
up   ʌp
us   ʌs
use (noun)   jus
uses (noun)   'jusɪz
use (verb)   juz
used   juzd
uses   'juzɪz
using   'juzɪŋ
used to (accustomed to)
      'justu
usually   'juʒʊəlɪ

V

vacation   ve'keʃən
vegetable   'vɛdʒtəbl
very   'vɛrɪ
Victor   'vɪktɚ
vinegar   'vɪnɪgɚ
visit   'vɪzɪt
visited   'vɪzɪtɪd
visitor   'vɪzɪtɚ
voice   vɔɪs

W

wait   wet
waited   'wetɪd
waiter   'wetɚ
waitress   'wetrɪs
walk   wɔk
walked   wɔkt
wall   wɔl
Walter   'wɔltɚ
want   wɑnt

wanted   'wɑntɪd
war   wɔr
warm   wɔrm
was   wʌz, wəz
wasn't   'wʌznt
wash   wɔʃ
Washington   'wɔʃɪŋtən
watch   wɑtʃ
watched   wɑtʃt
watches   'wɑtʃɪz
watchdog   'wɑtʃ,dɔg
water   'wɔtɚ
way   we
we   wi
wear   wɛr
    wore   wɔr
    worn   wɔrn
weather   'wɛðɚ
we'd   wid
Wednesday   'wɛnzdɪ
week   wik
well   wɛl
we'll   wil
we're   wɪr
were   wɝ
weren't   wɝnt
west   wɛst
western   'wɛstɚn
wet   wɛt
we've   wiv
what   hwɑt, hwʌt
whatever   hwət'ɛvɚ
wheel   hwil
when   hwɛn
whenever   hwɛn'ɛvɚ
where   hwɛr
wherever   hwɛr'ɛvɚ
whether   'hwɛðɚ
which   hwɪtʃ
whichever   hwɪtʃ'ɛvɚ
while   hwɑɪl

white   hwɑɪt
who   hu
whoever   hu'ɛvɚ
whom   hum
whose   huz
why   hwɑɪ
wide   wɑɪd
wider   'wɑɪdɚ
widest   'wɑɪdɪst
wife   wɑɪf
wives   wɑɪvz
will   wɪl
willing   'wɪlɪŋ
win   wɪn
    won   wʌn
wind (noun)   wɪnd
window   'wɪndo
windy   'wɪndɪ
winter   'wɪntɚ
wire   wɑɪr
wish   wɪʃ
wished   wɪʃt
wishes   'wɪʃɪz
with   wɪð
without   wɪð'ɑut
woman   'wumən
women   'wɪmɪn
wonderful   'wʌndɚfəl
won't   wont
word   wɝd
wore   wɔr
work   wɝk
worked   wɝkt
working   'wɝkɪŋ
worker   'wɝkɚ
worn   wɔrn
worse   wɝs
worst   wɝst
would   wud
wouldn't   'wudnt

write   raɪt
   wrote   rot
   written   'rɪtn
writing   'raɪtɪŋ
wrist watch   'rɪst,wɑtʃ
wrong   rɔŋ

Y

Yankees   'jæŋkɪz
yard   jɑrd
year   jɪr
yes   jɛs

yesterday   'jɛstɚdɪ
yet   jɛt
you   ju
you'd   jud
you'll   jul
young   jʌŋ
younger   'jʌŋgɚ
youngest   jʌŋgɪst
your   jʊr
you're   jʊr
yours   jʊrz
yourself   jʊr'sɛlf
yourselves   jʊr'sɛlvz
you've   juv

INDEX